The Story of Bawn by Katharine Tynan

Katherine Tynan was born on January 23rd 1859 into a large farming family in Clondalkin, County Dublin, and educated at a convent school in Drogheda. In her early years she suffered from eye ulcers, which left her somewhat myopic.

She first began to have her poems published in 1878. A great friend to Gerard Manley Hopkins and to WB Yeats (who it is rumoured proposed marriage but was rejected). With Yeats to encourage her, her poetry blossomed and she was equally supportive of his.

She married fellow writer and barrister Henry Albert Hinkson in 1898. They moved to England where she bore and began to raise 5 children although two were to tragically die in infancy.

In 1912 they returned to Claremorris, County Mayo when her husband was appointed magistrate there from 1912 until 1919. Sadly her husband died that year but Katherine continued to write.

Her output was prolific, some sources have her as the author of almost a 100 novels, many volumes of poetry, short stories, biography and many volumes which she edited.

Katherine died on April 2nd 1931 and she is buried at Kensal Green Cemetery in London.

Index of Contents
Chapter I - Myself
Chapter II - The Ghosts
Chapter III - The Creamery
Chapter IV - Richard Dawson
Chapter V - The Nurse
Chapter VI - One Side of a Story
Chapter VII - Old, Unhappy, Far-off Things
Chapter VIII - The Stile in the Wood
Chapter IX - A Rough Lover
Chapter X - The Trap
Chapter XI - The Friend
Chapter XII - The Enemy
Chapter XIII - Enlightenment
Chapter XIV - The Miniature
Chapter XV - The Empty House
Chapter XVI - The Portrait
Chapter XVII - The Will of Others
Chapter XVIII - Flight
Chapter XIX - The Crying in the Night
Chapter XX - An Eavesdropper
Chapter XXI - The New Maid
Chapter XXII - The Dinner Party
Chapter XXIII - The Bargain
Chapter XXIV - The Blow Falls
Chapter XXV - The Lover

Chapter XXVI - The Tribunal
Chapter XXVII - Brosna
Chapter XXVIII - The Quick and the Dead
Chapter XXIX - The Sickness
Chapter XXX - The Dark Days
Chapter XXXI - The Wedding Dress
Chapter XXXII - The New Home
Chapter XXXIII - The End of It
Chapter XXXIV - The Knocking at the Door
Chapter XXXV - The Messenger
Chapter XXXVI - The Old Lovers
Chapter XXXVII - The Judgment of God
Chapter XXXVIII - Confession
Chapter XXXIX - The Bridegroom Comes
Chapter XL - King Cophetua
KATHARINE TYNAN – A SHORT BIOGRAPHY
KATHARINE TYNAN – A CONCISE BIBLIOGRAPHY

CHAPTER I

MYSELF

I am Bawn Devereux, and I have lived as long as I remember at Aghadoe Abbey with my grandfather and grandmother, the Lord and Lady St. Leger.

At one time we were a family of five. There was my Uncle Luke, and there was my cousin Theobald.

Theobald was my boy cousin, and we played together up and down the long corridors in winter, and in the darkness of the underground passage, in summer in the woods and shrubberies and gardens, and we were happy together.

I was eager to please Theobald, and I put away from me my natural shrinkings from things he did not mind, lest he should despise me and be dissatisfied with me, longing for a boy's company. I would do all he did, and I must have been a famous tomboy. But my reward was that he never seemed to desire other company than mine.

Once, indeed, I remember that when he handed me live bait to put upon the hook I turned suddenly pale and burst into tears.

When I had done it I looked at him apprehensively, dreading to see his contempt written in his face, but there was no such thing. There was instead the dawn of a new feeling. My cousin's face wore such an expression as I had never seen in it before. He was at this time a tall boy of fifteen, and Bridget Connor, my grandmother's maid, was making me my first long frock.

He looked at me with that strange expression, and he said, "Poor little Bawn!"

It was the beginning of the new order of things in which I fagged for him no more, but was spared the labours and fatigues I had endured cheerfully during our early years. Indeed, I often wonder now at the things I did for him, such things as the feminine nature turns from with horror, although they seem to come naturally enough to a boy.

That day I heard my grandfather and grandmother discussing me.

Theobald was playing in a cricket match in the neighbourhood, and I was at home, reading in one of the recesses of the library. The book was Thackeray's "Henry Esmond," and I was so lost in the romance and tenderness of it, I was at that chapter where Harry returns bringing his sheaves with him, that I did not notice what they were saying till my own name caught my ears.

I remember that the afternoon had come on wet, and that while I read the wet branches of the lilac beat against the leaded window. I could see the flowers through an open pane, and smell their delightful perfume. There was an apple tree in view, too, with all its blossoms hanging in pink limpness.

I had forgotten my grandfather and grandmother sitting by the library fire, within the hooded settle that made the fireside like a little room; and they had forgotten my presence, if indeed they had known of it.

"Bawn is the very moral of what I was at her age," my grandmother said. "Have you noticed, Toby"—my grandfather also was a Theobald—"how tall she grows? And how she sways in walking like a poplar tree? She has my complexion before it ran in streaks, and my hair before it faded, and my eyes before they were dim. She has the carriage of the head which made them call me the Swan of Dunclody. She will be fifteen come Michaelmas, and she shall have my pearls for her neck."

I heard her in an excessive surprise. My grandmother had been esteemed a great beauty in her day and had been sung by the ballad-singers. Was it possible that my looks could be like hers? I had not thought about them hitherto any more than my cousin had about his. It was with almost a sense of relief that I heard my grandfather's reply.

"The child is well enough," he said, "but as for being so like you, that she is not, nor ever will have your share of beauty. As for your spoilt roses I do not see them, nor the dimmed eyes, nor the faded hair. You were lovely when I saw you first, and you are no less lovely in my sight to-day."

"In your sight—at seventy!" my grandmother said; and I could picture to myself the well-pleased expression of her dear face.

As for my Uncle Luke, of him I have but a dim memory, yet it is of something bonny. To be sure I have his picture in my grandmother's boudoir to remind me of him, a fair, full-lipped, smiling and merry face, with dark brown hair which would have curled if it were permitted. His comeliness survived even the hideous fashion of men's dress of his day, and my memory of him is of one in riding-breeches and a scarlet coat, for I think that must have been how I saw him oftenest.

He used to lift me to his shoulders and let me climb upon his head, and I remember that it seemed very fine to me to survey the world from that eminence.

I could have been no more than six years of age when my Uncle Luke vanished out of my surroundings.

At that time Theobald had not come to be an inmate of Aghadoe, and I noticed things as an over-wise child, accustomed to the society of its elders, will.

I often wondered about it in later years. I had no memory of a wake and a funeral, and I think if these things had been I should have known. But there was a period of trouble in which I was packed away to my nursery and the companionship of Maureen Kelly, our old nurse.

When I emerged from that it was to find my grandfather stern and sad, and my grandmother with a scared look and the roses of her cheeks faded.

And for long the shadow lay over Aghadoe. But in course of time people grew used to it as they will to all things, and my grandfather took snuff and played whist with his cronies, and drank his French claret, and rode to hounds, as he had been used; and my grandmother played on the harp to him of evenings when we were alone, and walked with him and talked to him, and saw to the affairs of her household, as though the machinery of life had not for a period run slow and heavy.

CHAPTER II

THE GHOSTS

We were very old-fashioned at Aghadoe Abbey and satisfied with old-fashioned ways. There was a great deal of talk about opening up the country, and even the gentry were full of it, but my grandfather would take snuff and look scornful.

"And when you have opened it up," he said, "you will let in the devil and all his angels."

It was certainly true that the people had hitherto been kind and innocent, so that any change might be for the worse, yet I was a little curious about what lay out in the world beyond our hills. And now it was no great journey to see, for they had opened a light railway, and from the front of the house we could see beyond the lake and the park, through the opening where the Purple Hill rises, that weird thing which rushes round the base of the hill half a dozen times a day before it climbs with no effort to the gorge between the hills and makes its way into the world. It does not even go by steam, so the thing was a great marvel to us and our people, to whom steam was quite marvel enough.

My grandfather at first would not even look on it. I have seen him turn away sharply from the window to avoid seeing it. When we went out to drive we turned our backs upon it, my grandfather saying that he would not insult his horses by letting them look at it, and indeed I think that, old as they were, yet having blood in them they would curvet a bit if they saw anything so strange to them.

There is one thing the light railway has done, and that is to give the people a market for their goods. We were all much poorer than we once were, except Mr. Dawson, who made his money by money-lending in Dublin and London; but even with Mr. Dawson's big house we did not make a market for the countryside.

Besides, there was a stir among the people there used not to be. They were spinning and weaving in their cottages, and they were rearing fowl and growing fruit and flowers.

The things which before the peasant children did for sport they now did for profit as well. It caused the greatest surprise in the minds of the people when they discovered that anybody could want their blackberries and their mushrooms; that money was to be made out of even the gathering of shamrocks. They thought that people out in the world who were ready to pay money for such things must be very queer people indeed. But since there were "such quare ould oddities," it was just as well, since they made life easier for the poor.

Another thing was that a creamery had been started at Araglin, only a mile or two from us, and the girls went there from the farms to learn the trade of dairying.

If it were not for the light railway none of these things would have been possible, and so I forgave it that it flew with a shriek round the base of the Purple Hill, setting all the mountains rattling with echoes, and disturbing the water fowl on the lakes and the song-birds in the woods, the eagle in his eyrie, and the wild red deer, to say nothing of the innumerable grouse and partridges and black cock and plover and hares and rabbits on the mountain-side.

My grandmother was not as angry against the light railway as my grandfather; she used to say that we must go with the times, and she was glad the people were stirring since it kept their thoughts from turning to America. She had been talked over by Miss Champion, my godmother and the greatest friend we have. And Miss Champion was always on the side of the people, and had even persuaded my grandmother to let her have some of her famous recipes, such as those for elder and blackberry wine, and for various preserves, and for fine soaps and washes for the skin, so that the people might know them and make more money.

"Everyone makes money except the gentry," my grandfather grumbled, "and we grow poorer year by year."

My grandfather talked freely in my presence; and I knew that Aghadoe Abbey was mortgaged to the doors and that the mortgages would be foreclosed at my grandfather's death. They kept nothing from me, and my grandmother has said to me with a watery smile: "If I survive your grandfather, Bawn, my dear, you and I will have to find genteel lodgings in Dublin. It would be a strange thing for a Lady St. Leger to come down from Aghadoe Abbey to that. To be sure there was once a Countess went ballad-singing in the streets of Cork."

"That day is far away," I answered. "And when it comes there will be no genteel lodgings, but Theobald and I will take care of you somewhere. In a little house it may be, but one with a garden where you can walk in the sun in winter mornings as you do now, and prod at the weeds in the path as you do now with your silver-headed cane."

"If I could survive your grandfather," she said, turning away her head, "my heart would break to leave Aghadoe. I ask nothing of you and Theobald, Bawn, but that you should take care of each other when we are gone. It is not right that the old should burden the young."

I have always known, or at least since I was capable of entertaining such things, that our grandparents destined Theobald and me for each other. I have no love for Theobald such as I find in my books, but I have a great affection for him as the dearest of brothers.

I have not said before that he is a soldier. What else should he be but a soldier? Since there have always been soldiers in the family, and my grandfather could not have borne him to be anything else.

Dear Theobald, how brave and simple and kind he was!

I have said nothing about the ghosts of Aghadoe Abbey, but it has many ghosts, or it had.

First and foremost there is the Lord St. Leger, who was killed in a Dublin street brawl a hundred years ago, who will come driving home at midnight headless in his coach, and the coachman driving him also headless, carrying his head under his arm. That is not a very pleasant thing to see enter as the gates swing open of themselves to let the ghost through.

Then there is the ghost of the woman who cries outside in the shrubbery. I have seen her myself in a glint of the moonlight, her black hair covering her face as she bends to the earth, incessantly seeking something among the dead leaves, which she cannot discover, and for which she cries.

And again, there is the lady who goes down the stairs, down, down, through the underground passage, and yet lower to the well that lies under the house, and is seen no more. A new maid once saw her in broad daylight, or at least in the grey of the morning, and followed her down the stairs, thinking that it was one of the family ill perhaps, who needed some attention. She could tell afterwards the very pattern of the lace on the fine nightgown, and describe how the fair curls clustered on the lady's neck. It was only when the lady disappeared before her, a white shimmer down the darkness of the underground corridor, that the poor thing realized she had seen a ghost, and fell fainting, with a clatter of her dustpan and brush which brought her help.

I could make a long list of the ghosts, for they are many, but I will not, lest I should be tedious. Only Aghadoe Abbey was eerie at night, especially in winter storms, since my cousin Theobald went away. I have often thought that the curious formation of the house, which has as many rooms beneath the ground as above it, helped to give it an eerie feeling, for one could not but imagine those downstair rooms filled with ghosts. I had seen the rooms lit dimly once or twice, but for a long time we had not used them, the expense of lighting them with a thousand wax candles glimmering in glittering chandeliers being too great.

But in the days before Cousin Theobald left us I was not afraid. He slept across the corridor from my room, and I had only to cry out and I knew he would fly to my assistance.

His sword was new at that time, and he was very proud of it. He turned it about, making it flash in the sunlight, and, said he, "Cousin Bawn, fear nothing; for if anything were to frighten you, either ghost or mortal, I would run it through with my sword. At your least cry I should wake, and I have always the sword close to my hand. Very often I lie awake when you do not think it to watch over you."

It gave me great comfort at the time, though looking back on it now I think my cousin, being so healthy and in the air all day, must have slept very soundly. Yet I am sure he thought he woke.

And, indeed, after he left the ghosts were worse than ever. I used to take my little dog into my arms for company, and, hiding my head under the bedclothes, I used to lie quaking because of the crying of the ghosts. It was a wild winter when Theobald left us, and they cried every night. It is a sound I have never grown used to, though I have heard it every winter I can remember. And also the swish of the satin as it went by my door, and the tap of high-heeled shoes. They cried more that winter than I ever heard them, except in the winter after Uncle Luke went away (but then I was little, and had the company of Maureen Kelly, my nurse); and in a winter which was yet to be.

But at that time I was happy despite the ghosts, and had no idea that the world held any fate for me other than to be always among such gentle, high-minded people as were my grandfather and grandmother, my cousin Theobald, and my dear godmother. For ghosts, especially of one's own blood, are gentle and little likely to harm one, and must be permitted by the good God to come back for some good reason.

It is another matter when it is some one of flesh and blood, who wants to take you in his arms and kiss you while your flesh creeps, and your whole soul cries out against it. And it is the worst matter of all when those to whom you have fled all your days for help and protection, to whom you would have looked to save you from such a thing, look on, with pale faces indeed, yet never interfere.

Often, often in the days that were to come I had rather be of the company of the ghosts than to endure the things I had to endure.

CHAPTER III

THE CREAMERY

It was through my godmother that I went to learn the butter-making at the Creamery, and since it was strange that my grandparents should have permitted me to go, I must explain how it was that Miss Champion came to have so much influence with them and over our affairs generally, and who the lady was.

She was our nearest neighbour, at Castle Clody, the beautiful old house which stands on the side of the river Clody, overlooking the falls. She had been an orphan almost from her birth, and had grown up as independent and able to manage her affairs as any man.

She was a great sportswoman even in our country of such, and being exposed to all manner of wind and weathers, her face had come to have a weather-beaten look. She had very beautiful grey eyes and a deal of black, silken hair, and she was unusually tall. Even the weather, when it had roughened and tanned her complexion, had but given her a new charm to my mind, for she looked as wholesome and sweet and out-of-doors as the weather itself. Yet people said she was plain. I could not see it, but then she was too good to me and I loved her.

I remember that usually she wore grey tweed tailor-made gowns, in which her beautiful figure showed to advantage, unless she happened to be riding when she wore a dark grey habit. But I have seen her very splendid when she went out in the evening; and I have never seen a woman better fitted to grace splendid garments.

She had taken to herself at Castle Clody, because it was her nature to foster and protect something, a cousin of hers, a peevish, exacting invalid whom we always called Miss Joan, her name being Joan Standish.

If you spent only ten minutes by Miss Joan's bedside you were sure to hear her grumble at her cousin Mary. Since everything was done for her that could possibly be done for an invalid her lot had great alleviations, but she seemed to take it as an offence that my godmother should be so strong and free, should walk with such a swinging stride, and always enjoy her food, and bring that smell of the open air with her wherever she came.

She had an unpleasant flattering way with her at times.

"Come, my dear," she would say, "sit down and talk to me. I live in so dreary an isolation, and my nerves get into that state that I could scream when a harsh voice falls on my ear. Your voice is soft and sweet, but have you ever noticed Mary's? It is as harsh as a crow's, and when she comes in with those strong boots of hers creaking she destroys my peace of mind for an hour."

"She has a beautiful voice," I answered her once, "and there is such assurance in her tread. I should think it would be more trying to the nerves to live where every one went tiptoe."

But no manner of coldness could check Miss Joan's propensity for belittling her benefactress. And I remember that once she had been tittle-tattling as usual, and had said something more indefensible than usual of her benefactress, when looking up suddenly we found Miss Champion in the room.

"Let the child love me, Joan," she said, with the nearest approach to sharpness I ever heard in her speech; but when Miss Joan burst into tears she stooped and shook up her pillows and soothed her in a way that was tender without being attached, and afterwards she said something to me which was a dark saying since I did not know the secret between her and Miss Joan.

"One must needs be good to anything that has hurt one so much," she said.

I had always known vaguely that there was something between Mary Champion and my Uncle Luke, and that explained to some extent her influence with my grandparents. She brought into their shut-up lives, indeed, the open air and the ways of other folk, without which I think we should have all grown too strange and odd and a century at least behind our time. Indeed, even with her, I think we were so much out of date.

"The child grows more and more like a plant which has lived without the light," she said one day of me to my grandmother.

"It is Bawn's nature to look pale," my grandmother said, looking at me in an alarmed way.

"It is her nature to look pale perhaps," my godmother said, while I fidgeted at hearing myself discussed, "but she ought to look no paler than this apple-blossom I am wearing, which at all events dreams of rose-colour. You keep her too much penned. I shall have to carry her off to Dublin for some gaiety. If the season were not nearly over—"

"We couldn't do without Bawn," said my grandmother hastily. "We are too old to live without something young beside us. Besides, she is very happy—aren't you, Bawn?"

"Very happy." I answered the appeal in her dear voice and eyes. And to be sure I was happy, if it were not for the loneliness and the ghosts at night.

"She is always reading," my godmother went on. "Young girls should not be always reading. It bends their backs and dims their eyes and makes them forget their walks and rides. I'll tell you what, Lady St. Leger, you had better let Bawn come and learn butter-making with me at the Creamery. I am going to take a course of lessons and then I can make my own butter. I think Margaret Dwyer is getting past her work. Joan says the butter is rancid, and for once I believe Joan has cause. Every lady ought to at least superintend her own dairy."

"I used to visit mine often," said my grandmother, "before Lord St. Leger needed so much of my time. It was a pretty place, with white walls and a fountain bubbling. It is a long time since I have visited it."

"Let Bawn do it. I went to visit Lady Ardaragh the other day, and she gave me tea in her dairy. It is coming into fashion to be housekeepers and dairymaids once more."

"Would you like to go to the Creamery, Bawn?" asked my grandmother.

"I should love to," said I. "And to have a herd of little Kerries like Lady Ardaragh. The dairy is as pretty as ever, but it wants washing, and the fountain is broken. I believe Michael Friely could mend it."

My grandfather made no objection when he heard of the plan, only saying something with a laugh about fine ladies liking to play dairymaids. So it was settled I should go to the Creamery; and Bridget Connor made gowns of cotton for me to wear at the Creamery, and white aprons to go with them.

I think my grandmother looked on it as a child's play for my diversion, and she would have Bridget make me as pretty as she could. I dare say I did look as though I played at work, for I caught sight of myself in the Venetian mirror on the wall of my grandmother's boudoir as she turned me round about, her maid, Bridget Connor, who learnt dressmaking in Paris, pinching here and letting loose there.

The walls of my grandmother's boudoir are covered with mother-of-pearl which glows splendidly when the lamps are lit.

I glanced at the Venetian mirror and saw myself like a rose in my rosy frock, with the apron of spotless muslin and the mushroom hat with a wreath of pink roses. My grandmother said something about dairying at the Petit Trianon, but indeed my intentions were of the most business-like.

I remember that it was the month of May, and all the pastures were richest gold and snowiest white, drifts of gold and white. The thorn-trees were all in bloom, and the banks were covered with the white stitchwort and blue speedwell. The birds were in full song, and the mornings and evenings were especially delicious.

I was to attend the Creamery for three months, so as to become proficient in dairymaid work, and then I thought I could do some good among our own people who could not afford to send a girl to the Creamery to learn her business. Or it might be where there was no girl, and the vanithee-that is to say, the good woman—did her work in her own way, not half pressing the water out of the butter, so that it became rancid after a few hours, or letting the cream become rancid before she churned it. I had hopes that I could persuade even the most obstinate of them to mend their ways; and that perhaps was an indication of my youth.

CHAPTER IV

RICHARD DAWSON

I used to go to Araglin every day, wet or dry. It is about three miles from the Abbey as one goes to it through our own park, and by Daly's Wood, which is a little wood, barely more than a coppice; the entrance to it faces a gate in our park wall, and when you have traversed its short length you have cut off a mile of the distance to Araglin if you went by road.

I liked the work at the Creamery extremely. The place was so cool and sweet with the splashing of falling water and the smell of cream and warm milk, and the fresh-looking, wholesome girls in their print frocks, and all the shining, clean utensils.

The walk to and from the Creamery was most delightful, especially those May days when there were such drifts of flowers and the wood was full of bluebells, and little white and blue wild anemones and harebells and sweet woodruff.

Nothing could well be more fragrant than the wood in those days of early summer.

It was a place in which the trees were of the light and springing variety with slender, pale trunks, but high overhead a mass of feathery leaves made a roof against the sky.

I have often sheltered in the wood from a heavy shower and not received a drop; yet it was suffused through the sunshiny hours with a soft goldenness. Below the trees was only undergrowth and the grass sown thickly with flowers. The path went so straight through it that as you entered by the stile at one end you saw far before you the arch of light over the stile that took you on to the road at the other end.

Occasionally my godmother was at the Creamery, working away with the rest, but she had so much to do of many kinds that she could not be looked for regularly.

In a little while I was very much at home among the girls, who at first were shy of me. If I could have gone to the Creamery at Araglin without their knowing that I was Bawn Devereux, the young lady at the big house, I would have enjoyed it, but that was not possible.

However, they soon forgot to be afraid of me, and laughed and chattered among themselves, very little deterred by my presence, except for giving me a shy glance now and again. They were most polite and gentle with me, and would help me if they saw me lifting a heavy crock of milk, with a "By your leave, Miss Bawn," which was very pleasant.

I used to listen to their simple talk after they had forgotten their awe of me, and smile and sigh to myself. It was often of lovers, and they rallied each other about this or that swain; and sometimes it was of their fortunes, which were being built up by tiny sums out of much poverty, so that their milk and roses, their bright eyes and satin heads might be gilt for their cold lovers. But I never heard anything Lady St. Leger would not wish me to hear; indeed, the talk those summer days was in keeping with the freshness and sweetness of the world about us.

One day that we were butter-making a party of visitors came in to see the Creamery, as sometimes happened. I was washing the butter which lay before me in a pan of water, with the sleeves of my gown pinned above my elbow.

When the visitors paused to see what we were doing I did not look at them but went on with my work. There was a good deal of whispering and laughing among them, and I felt without looking at them that they were not gentle-folk, at least such gentle-folk as I knew.

But presently I had the most painful sense of being stared out of countenance, and lifting my eyes I found the eyes of one of the visitors fixed upon me with so rude and insolent a gaze that the colour rushed into my cheeks as though someone had struck me.

The person was a youngish man, dressed in what I took to be the height of fashion. We know little enough about fashion, and my grandfather's knee-breeches and frilled shirt were very smart in the Forties. The young man had red hair and very bold blue eyes; his complexion was ruddy, and his strong white teeth showed under his red moustache.

At the moment of looking at him I was aware of the greatest aversion and fear within myself. I lowered my eyes and devoted myself to what I was doing, painfully conscious all the time of the colour in my cheeks which must make me conspicuous to those who were looking at me. I heard a little giggle; then the voice of one of the ladies very slightly subdued—

"Oh, come away, Dick. Don't you see how you are making that poor girl blush?"

To my relief I heard them go, but it was some time before I could recover myself.

I had no idea at all but that they were chance visitors brought into the neighbourhood by the light railway, but I was soon to be disillusioned.

Several times that day I caught the eyes of a very pretty and innocent-looking girl, named Nora Brady, fixed on me, and there was something odd about her look; so much so that later in the day, as I was putting on my hat to go home, while Nora was preparing to start without any such formality, I suddenly asked her—

"Why have you been looking at me now and again to-day as though you were going to say something to me?"

To my amazement she blushed hotly and stammered something about not having known that she was looking at me.

"Never mind, Nora," I said, pitying her confusion; "a cat may look at a king, you know. Not that I'm a king nor a queen either."

"Oh, indeed, Miss Bawn," she said, blushing again. "You're pretty enough to be the Queen. Sure that's why poor Master Richard stared at you, not meaning to be impudent at all, let alone that he thought you a poor girl."

"Master Richard?"

"Master Richard Dawson. 'Twas him came in to-day with some of the quality ladies they have stopping at Damerstown. He didn't mean any harm, Miss Bawn."

So it was Richard Dawson, the only son of the rich money-lender, on whom we of the older, more exclusive gentry turn our backs. He had been wild in his boyhood, and had quarrelled with his father and flung himself off to America. We had not heard of his return.

I noticed half consciously the pleading look of Nora's blue eyes under their black lashes. Why was the child so much concerned at what had offended me? But I hardly thought of her.

I was thinking with an unreasonable wave of repulsion that I should doubtless meet Richard Dawson, if not in the drawing-rooms of our friends at least about our quiet lanes and roads, where hitherto there had been nothing to fear. I wished he had stayed in America; and on one subject I made up my mind. That was that if I must meet Richard Dawson I should certainly be as cold to him as was compatible with civility to those in whose houses I might meet him.

For we were not all a century behind our times. Some of us had a Dublin season every year and had been presented at Court, and some of us even went to London for the season.

Lady Ardaragh was one of those. She used to quiz us openly for our old-fashioned ways, but so sweetly that even my grandmother laughed with her. And she used to say that if one were too particular about one's visiting-list so as to exclude the newly rich people, one would have to mark off half Park Lane and that wonderful district which she would have us believe lay all about it. One met the oddest people in her drawing-room, where she fluttered about among them like a gay little butterfly while Sir Arthur, her serious husband, locked himself away among his books.

"If I hadn't such oddities I should bore myself to extinction, dear Lady St. Leger," she said to my grandmother once. "Arthur will keep me here nine months of the year. What is one to do?"

"Why, I am sure there is plenty to do," my grandmother replied simply. "Bawn is busy from morning to night, what with her garden and her birds and her dogs and her reading and music, and now with the Creamery. So should I be if Lord St. Leger did not claim so much of my attention. I neglect things sadly nowadays because my husband leans on me as a staff, although I am nearly as old as he. And there is your dear boy."

Lady Ardaragh frowned.

"Sir Arthur never knows how I look, what I put on," she said. "He was an ardent lover enough, but now I do not think I could provoke him if I tried. He simply does not think of me. An illuminated manuscript is more to him than I am; and he would rather have a black-letter book than my youth. As for my Robin, I adore him; but his fine nurse comes between him and me. And to be sure, even if she didn't I have no time for babies."

That was the way with Lady Ardaragh. Her moods changed from one minute to another with incredible swiftness.

I had always had a great admiration for her, the pretty creature, and when she had spoken of the illuminated manuscript I had a sudden vision of her with her head of curls, and her pink, babyish face against a background of pale gold.

To be sure her diversions, as even I knew, were something of the talk of the countryside; and I have heard ladies say when they visited my grandmother that it was a wonder Sir Arthur permitted it, but they would be silent when they saw me. Yet my grandmother loved Lady Ardaragh, and before my presence was noticed I have heard her say in a rebuking way that her ladyship's ways were only the ways of a girl married to an elderly, grave scholar.

I was tolerably sure that some time or other we should meet the Dawsons in Lady Ardaragh's drawing-room, and I looked forward with horror to seeing Richard Dawson again.

But as it chanced, I was to meet him otherwise, and in no very pleasant fashion.

CHAPTER V

THE NURSE

It was a few days later that, coming in one afternoon, I found Miss Champion with my grandmother and noticed that there was something odd in the manner of both of them. Nor was I kept long in suspense about it, for Miss Champion, who was the most candid person alive, could not long keep a secret.

"Would you like to go to Dublin, Bawn?" she asked.

To Dublin! I could hardly have been more bewildered if she had asked me would I like to go to the North Pole. Indeed, I had never contemplated going so far. It would have been a great adventure to have gone even so far as Quinn, our fair and market town, which lies on the other side of the Purple Hill, seven miles away.

I stammered out that I should like to go to Dublin, looking from Mary Champion's face to my grandmother's, for I could hardly believe that the latter would consent to so tremendous an adventure.

"It is time for her to see and be seen," my godmother went on. "You are twenty years old, are you not, Bawn? Why, at twenty I had seen a deal of the world, had travelled far away from Castle Clody and the valley of the Moy. Next season she ought to be presented, Lady St. Leger. I shall take her up and do it myself, if you will not. She ought not to be hidden away."

At this my grandmother looked alarmed, and said something under her breath of which I caught but a name or two, my Uncle Luke's and Theobald's.

From whatever my grandmother had said Miss Champion seemed to dissent even violently.

"It is all forgotten," she said, "and if any remembered it they would take my view of it and not yours. He should have stayed and faced it out. No jury would have brought in a worse verdict than manslaughter, and if it had been tried outside Dublin, in Irish Ireland, no jury would have convicted at all. I know the people adore Luke's memory because he struck that blow in defence of a woman. Why will you behave as though you held him guilty, Lady St. Leger?"

She gained heat as she proceeded, and although she spoke hastily, and hardly above her breath I heard every word.

It was not the first indication I had had that my Uncle Luke's disappearance was connected somehow with a deed of violence, although the details had never been told to me. Now I spoke up.

"I am sure that Uncle Luke did nothing we need be ashamed of, Gran," I said. "I remember him well, and he was very kind. I can see him now putting my canary's little leg in splints when it had broken it, and the dogs adored him. Old Dido yet listens for his return."

My grandmother began to weep softly.

"I did not want Bawn to know anything about those dreadful happenings, Mary," she said. "And whatever I believe or feel about Luke would not stand in the eyes of the law, since I am only his mother and why should I not believe in my son?"

"It is my quarrel with you and Lord St. Leger that you will act as though you believed him guilty," my godmother said. "As for Bawn, Lady St. Leger, you must let me tell her the story. It is time that she should know it. Not now, but another time when it will not grieve you. And you will let her come with me to Dublin?"

"If her grandfather consents, Mary. I have no doubt that he will consent if you ask him. But Bawn will need some clothes if she is to see your friends. What are we going to do about her clothes?"

"You must leave that to me, Lady St. Leger, as being Bawn's godmother. If I have not done my duty by her hitherto, it does not mean that I never shall."

After all, I did not hear Uncle Luke's story from my godmother but from Maureen Kelly.

Maureen was now getting old, and she had a room allotted to herself at the extreme end of the left wing which looked out on the gable of the Abbey and the graves which are all that remain of the old Abbey from which the house takes its name.

To be sure the grass grows up to the empty window-sockets of the gable; and as for the graves they are clean blotted out in the prairie grass that is like the grey waves of the sea above them.

It is a narrow slip of a room, and she sits there and sews, mending the linen which is old and thin and darning finely the holes in the damask cloth or the rents which time has made in my grandmother's lace; and when the light fails her knitting those stockings of fine blue-grey wool which my grandfather always wears.

Maureen, as often happens with old privileged servants, quarrels with the other servants and is not much sought after by them. She lives in a great independence of her own, and has her own cups and saucers; they are fine old china, with brown sea-shells and seaweed upon them, and they belonged to the nursery when I was the one child there.

And she has her own tea and bread and butter and sugar; and anything else she requires she fetches from the kitchen, walking about haughtily among the other servants, and not staying longer than is necessary to get what things she requires.

I went very often to Maureen's room.

For one thing, it was like looking into my childhood to go there. It is so still. The nursery pictures are on the wall, and in a cupboard there are my discarded books and toys, with others of an earlier date than mine. There is the dolls' house which was given to my great-grandmother when she was a child by Lord Kilwarden, that just judge who was a great friend of our family. It is not so elaborate as the dolls' houses of to-day, but it is big enough for a small child to creep within it, and it seemed wonderful to me as it had done to my mother before me, and to my Aunt Eleanor, who was Theobald's mother. I know my grandmother loves the dolls' house, and would not consent to its being put away in the lumber-room.

In winter Maureen's room is the warmest spot of the house, which is old and draughty, and I have always gone there when I have wanted to get the chill out of my bones. Maureen will sit by the window sewing, while I get down on to the little stool which used to be mine in my childhood and look into the heart of the flame and imagine things there.

There is a photograph of my Uncle Luke on the chimney-piece, an artless thing of a country photographer. He is wearing his militia uniform, and even the country photographer had no power to destroy the bonny charm which sat on his eyes and his lips.

Now Maureen had, whether from increasing years or from the lonely life she led, come to have delusions at times, to mix up me with my mother or my Aunt Eleanor, to talk of Uncle Luke as though he were yet with us or might be expected at any moment home from college, or from a hunting day or a fair or market, or his training with his regiment on the Curragh of Kildare.

But on this day she was clear enough in her mind.

Uncle Luke's old setter, Dido, that was a young thing when he went away, had followed me upstairs and lay along the rug with her head on my lap. Now and again she pricked her ears as though she heard something or thought she did. It was Dido who led us on to talk of Uncle Luke. Maureen is no more tolerant of dogs about her than others of her class, but she tolerates Dido because she belonged to Uncle Luke.

"If his Lordship had a real kindness for that old dog," she began, "he'd poison her and put her out of her trouble."

Dido looked back over her ears at her as a dog will, knowing itself discussed.

"I don't think Dido would call it a kindness, Maureen," said I. "Let me see—how old is she?"

"She must be nigh on fifteen years old. I remember well the day Master Luke brought her home. I wonder his Lordship can bear to have her about, seeing who it was that gave her to him."

"And who was it, Maureen?" I asked.

Her old eyes narrowed themselves cunningly.

"No one could ever say, Miss Bawn, that I talked about the family."

"Very well, Maureen," I said. "But I am to hear it, all the same. Miss Champion is going to tell me. She said so to my grandmother yesterday, and would have done it then only that she feared to disturb Gran. I am going to her this afternoon to talk about our trip to Dublin, and then she will tell me."

"That is the way," said Maureen, with great bitterness. "People will tell you not to tell things: and when you've held yourself in till you're fit to burst after all those years they'll tell themselves. Why shouldn't you know, Miss Bawn, my lamb? There's some for Master Luke and there's some against him, but I'm for him whatever story was the true one."

"So should I be, Maureen," said I. "I remember how he carried me round the stables and to the kennels on his shoulder, and how he brought me in to see Bridget Kinsella, the huntsman's wife, and she gave me bread and brown sugar with cream over it. And when we were coming back it was cold, and Uncle Luke carried me inside his coat."

"Aye," said Maureen, "he was ever softhearted. A bit wild, but not more so than became his station. And if Miss Champion had been kinder with him the trouble need never have happened."

I had often noticed a curious hostility in Maureen towards Miss Champion, and had wondered at it, since she was so devoted to us all.

"She tell the story, indeed!" she went on with bitterness. "If she tells it she'd better keep back nothing. Why did she send him to get consolation from other ladies? He was always true-hearted from a child. And if Miss Cardew had a fancy for him, who should blame her?"

Now, I had heard dimly of Miss Cardew who was an heiress, and of how Sir Jasper Tuite had tried to abduct her, but somehow I had never heard the whole of the story. People had dropped talking about it as soon as they had discovered my presence. And I had had no idea at all that it had to do with Uncle Luke.

CHAPTER VI

ONE SIDE OF A STORY

"Tell me now, Maureen," I said, "since you have told me so much. It was Sir Jasper Tuite, was it not, that waylaid Miss Cardew on her way from Kilmany Church, and was killed in the struggle? And what had Uncle Luke to do with it?"

"Ah, that is what only he himself could tell. For the poor young lady, who was never over-strong, went clean out of her wits afterwards: and to be sure Sir Jasper Tuite was dead and cold when they found him. The horses that drew the carriage had taken flight and galloped off home with Miss Cardew, and her cowardly coachman had run away and never came back till the whole thing was over. Miss Cardew, poor thing, never could tell what happened, rightly. And Sir Jasper, if he was dead, he hadn't died of the pistol-shot, but of an old trouble of the heart. The bullet was in the fleshy part of his shoulder, and the doctors would have got it out as easy as possible. And, sure, if he'd lived he'd have been sent to prison. It used to be life for runnin' away with a lady against her will in the old days. Master Luke's pistol was found just as he'd thrown it down, and his name on it. He must have thought he'd killed Sir Jasper. Small wrong, some people say, if he had, for Sir Jasper was bad as many a poor girl knew to her cost."

"Uncle Luke should not have gone away," I said.

"Well, you see, dearie, he thought it the kindest thing to do. And then—there were stories. I never believed them myself. People asked how it was that Master Luke came to be armed. There was reason enough, for the country was disturbed at the time."

"Stories," I repeated after her—"what stories?"

"Why, there were some bad enough to say that it was Master Luke was tryin' to abduct the lady, and that it was Sir Jasper was hinderin' him. I couldn't believe it myself. He cared for none but Miss Mary, although she'd been hard to him. And Miss Irene Cardew would have gone with Master Luke willin' enough. A pretty delicate little lady she was, and 'ud jump if she caught sight of her own shadow. Sure, Master Luke could have nothing but pity for her."

"There seem to have been a great many stories," I said.

"Aye, indeed, so there were, my jewel. There isn't two you'd meet in the county this minute 'ud hold the same opinion about it. Not but that any way the country people are on the side of Master Luke."

I was silent for a few minutes, stroking Dido's silky head, letting her rippled ears fall through my fingers. Her dim eyes were fixed on me with a terrible wistfulness, as though she longed to speak and could not. I felt a great pity for the old dog. What a sad lot is theirs, depending on our presence as they do for the light in their sky, to whom our slightest absence is the absence of death.

"Was nothing ever heard of him?" I asked after that silence.

"Nothing. Some said that he got on board a hooker and was carried to Liverpool and got off to America. Others said the same hooker—she was a stranger in these parts—was swept out to sea and, in the big storm that broke that very week, foundered."

"It is most likely," said I, "for if he were living he would never have left them in suspense all these years."

"There, you're wrong, Miss Bawn. Master Luke is not dead."

Dido stirred uneasily and whimpered.

"He's not dead, Miss Bawn, for if he was dead the banshee would have cried. And the dead coach would have driven up with a rattle and stopped at our door. It never has, Miss Bawn. What you've heard has never stopped at our doors. To hear wheels in the distance is nothing. As for the cryin' in the shrubbery, that is another story. Some day I may tell it to you, child."

"You have not told me yet," I said, "why you blame my godmother."

I had it in my mind that Lord and Lady St. Leger did not blame her, so there could be nothing to blame. It was some stupid and ignorant prejudice of old Maureen's. I knew she had fostered my Uncle Luke, and that she loved him, as the foster-mother does, with an unreasoning and jealous passion.

Her old lips met tightly.

"Ask Miss Mary herself about that, Miss Bawn," she said. "No one can say that I am one to talk. After all those years, it would be a pity to spoil all the tellin' for Miss Mary."

She sat smiling to herself, a bitter and mocking smile, when she had finished the sentence. I knew Maureen better than to try to win talk from her when she had once made up her mind to silence, so I let her be, only changing the conversation to another subject.

"What will it be like, Maureen, when I am gone?" I asked.

"It will be lonely, Miss Bawn," she answered; and then, as I had expected, she added, with a little sourness, "Not that you are a patch on Master Luke and Miss Eleanor and your own mother for cheerfulness in the house. Och, the days I could tell of when there was the fine company-keepin', and the diversion, and the carriages of the quality drivin' up to the doors, and the music and the dancin'! Them were the days that were worth havin', an' not these days when everyone is old—everyone but yourself, Miss Bawn; and you're that quiet that I wouldn't know you were in the house. Och, the good days! the good days!"

"They were good when Theobald was here," I said. "He made enough noise, Maureen; didn't he? You used to scold then because he made so much."

"I always thought more of a boy than a girl," she answered. "You're bonny enough, Miss Bawn, but you're not to be compared with Master Theobald, let alone them I nursed at my breast—Master Luke and your mother and your Aunt Eleanor."

"Mary Cashel thinks the world of me," I said, with enjoyment. Mary Cashel is my foster-mother, and lives at the head of the Glen.

"She's a poor, foolish, talkative creature," Maureen said. "If her Ladyship had listened to me she'd never have had Mary Cashel in the house."

Just then the setting sun glinted on the windows of Brosna, the great house that neighbours ours, which belongs to the Cardews, and has been empty, as its owner, Anthony Cardew, has been away from it many years. The sun was going down in a great glory, and window after window in the long house-front took fire and flamed like a torch.

"You would think," said I, "that they were lighting fires over there against Captain Cardew's return."

Maureen rose from her place and peered curiously in the direction of my gaze.

"I wonder he doesn't be selling it," she said, "and not be letting it go to rack and ruin and him never comin' home. 'Tis an unlucky country so it is where the houses of the gentry must be all stannin' empty or tumblin' to ruins, or bein' turned into asylums or the like."

"I should like to see the inside of Brosna," I said. "Is it as fine as they say?"

"It is the finest house in this country, Miss Bawn—finer even than the Abbey. But all goin' to rack and ruin for want of an owner to look after it. But as for seein' it, I wouldn't be talkin' about such a thing. It is a long time since his Lordship and her Ladyship could bear to hear the name of Cardew."

"I have heard you say, Maureen," I went on, "that Anthony Cardew was the handsomest young man ever seen in this country, that he had a leg and foot as elegant even as Uncle Luke's, and that to see him dance was the finest sight you could wish for, and that all the ladies were in love with him."

"I never put him before Master Luke. No, no, Miss Bawn, I never put him before my own boy. There, don't be talkin' about the Cardews, child. What are they to you?"

I got up and went out; and while my thoughts were busy with my visit to Dublin there would flash through them like warp and woof the thought of Anthony Cardew, who had gone away before I was born and of whom so many romantic stories were told. I felt that I must hear some of them, even though the name of Cardew was not to be mentioned in our hearing.

CHAPTER VII

OLD, UNHAPPY, FAR-OFF THINGS

I found my godmother watering her rose trees on the eastward side of the house from which the sun had now departed. The grassy terraces before the house smelt deliciously, for a water-sprinkler in the grass sent out fine spray like a fountain. It was very hot weather, and I had walked across; it had been cool enough in the shelter of the wood but the roads had been blinding hot.

"Sit down, Bawn," she said, coming towards me, having left her hose to run at the foot of a rose tree. "See how busy I am! Of course, a gardener's boy would do it but I love to give drink to the thirsty."

She was wearing a cool muslin dress transparent at the neck. Round her throat she had a slender chain with a locket to it. She was brown as a berry, but she looked as though the hot weather dealt gently with her. As she sat down by me and took Dido's head into her lap, to the great discomfort of a rabble of jealous dogs who sat round watching her and whining, it struck me that her eyes were the very colour of the dog's and as faithful.

"You look cool," I said.

"And you; you have no idea how pink print becomes you. But first we will have tea. Joan has a sick headache and will have none of me to-day. So we shall be just our two selves."

As she said it I noticed a line of pain and weariness deepen in her forehead, and her lips droop ever so slightly. It was something I had noticed before when Miss Standish had been more than commonly trying. I looked at my godmother with new interest, having learnt what had befallen Uncle Luke. She wore her hair in an old-fashioned way which became her. It was in loops each side of her forehead, displaying her ears, and was then taken up and plaited at the back of her head. The fashion was a quarter of a century old but nothing could have been prettier.

She took Dido's head between her hands and looked down into her eyes.

"She is growing very old, Bawn," she said sadly.

It reminded me of something Maureen had said and had not explained.

"Who gave Dido to Uncle Luke?" I asked.

She turned red and pale.

"What have you been hearing, Bawn?" she asked.

"Maureen has been talking to me about Uncle Luke. I did not think it wrong to listen to her, since I knew that I was to hear the story from you."

"Maureen did not spare me," she said in a low voice.

"For the matter of that she said nothing. She hinted that you had been hard on Uncle Luke, but she bid me ask yourself."

"Do you think it likely I was hard to him, Bawn?"

She was looking into the dog's eyes now and the dog into hers. The two hearts that were always faithful to Uncle Luke understood each other. Deep answered deep.

"I am sure you were not," I said.

"Maureen did not know," she went on gently.

"Sure your dog for you could die
With no truer heart than I,"

she murmured, with a fervour that startled me. Then her eyes grew misty.

"Dido and I are always listening for the same foot," she said. "If Luke L'Estrange were to come back now, perhaps we should both die of joy. What was it you were asking me, Bawn? Who was it gave Luke the dog. It was Irene Cardew, poor girl. All the tragedy is over and done. I don't mind telling you, Bawn—Irene is beyond being hurt by it—that she was fond of Luke. Perhaps it was my fault. Luke had hurt me and I was angry, saying to myself that I did well to be angry. We never do well to be angry, little Bawn, with those we love. I thought there was plenty of time for Luke to come back and be forgiven. But there is never plenty of time in this world. I am sure of one thing, that he loved only me."

"And that is a great thing to be sure of," I said.

A servant brought out the tea-table and set it before us. We were silent while he went to and fro bringing us the tea equipage, the bread and butter and sandwiches and hot tea-cakes. When we were again alone my godmother poured out the tea, smiling at me across the cups.

"We must not talk any more of the old, unhappy, far-off things," she said. "You have heard enough, little Bawn; only take warning by the sins and follies of your elders. Do not quarrel with Theobald, thinking there is time to make up."

"For the matter of that," I said, "I never feel inclined to quarrel with Theobald. And, dear godmother, I am sure you were not hard with Uncle Luke."

"Thank you, Bawn. He was foolish like other young men of his class. I had better tell you, lest you should wrong Luke in your thoughts. He came to me when he had drunk too much. I thought I did well for his own sake to be angry and I sent him away unforgiven. There were many ready to comfort him, and it was not in him to rebuff a woman, especially a woman who let him see that she was in love with him. He was often with Irene Cardew while I was angry with him. It gave colour to the stories afterwards."

"I know; Maureen told me."

"No one that knew him could believe it. It was like Jasper Tuite that he could not even die without wronging another."

CHAPTER VIII

THE STILE IN THE WOOD

After that she changed the conversation to other things; and when I had drunk my tea and eaten with an appetite I went upstairs with her to see things she had promised to show me.

I had had no idea that they were for me. I knew that she had a great many old and beautiful things, and from my childhood I had delighted in them. I could remember her calling for me in her pony phaeton before Uncle Luke had left us, and she would carry me all over Castle Clody for she was a tall, strong young woman; and while she changed her dress I used to sit in the middle of her bed with the curtains of blue and silver damask falling to either side of me, and she would give me boxes of pretty things to play with. To this day I like better than any of her valuable jewels her pretty trinkets of garnet and amethyst and topaz, of which she has a great many. They lay in trays in glass-lidded boxes and I delighted to look at them. Many of them have come to me as Christmas and birthday gifts since then, and Miss Standish had many of them, for although she was an invalid she delighted in pretty things and was greedy for them. My dear godmother is one to give with both hands; indeed, to value things chiefly for the pleasure of giving them.

Lying on her bed now were a number of garments so pretty that I cried out in delight. They were all white, yellowed a little with age, and in some instances with a pattern in colours.

There was a scarf of China crêpe, powdered as thickly as possible with roses and golden bees. There was an opera cloak made of a beautiful old Indian shawl. There were several frocks of silk and lace and muslin and fine woollen. There were finely laced and frilled petticoats and silk stockings and shoes with paste buckles and a feather fan. Also there were fichus and lace-edged handkerchiefs and such things, to strike a young girl dumb with delight.

"They are all for you, Bawn," she said, smiling at me. "They were my wedding clothes, and they have lain packed away in silver paper all these years. I have brought them into the light of day for you. They ought to have been kept for your wedding perhaps, but as there is nothing definite—"

"Theobald and I shall be quite old before we need think of marriage, if we ever do," I said. "I don't want to be married. It is nicer when people will be satisfied with being just dear brothers. And are they really for me, god-mamma? Why should you not wear them yourself? They are so beautiful!"

"Let me have the pleasure of seeing you wear them, Bawn. We shall depend less on the Dublin shops during our visit. Louise will fit the things on you. They will have to be taken in for you. They will not look old-fashioned. The fashion has come back to them."

I stood an hour or more while Louise pinned the things on me, kneeling by my side and turning me this way and that way to look at myself in the long glass of the wardrobe.

She kept up a running conversation on the things while she fitted me; ecstatic little cries of admiration; deep sighs of satisfaction; with all the animation of the Frenchwoman.

"I believe you get at least as much pleasure out of them as I do, Louise," I said.

"Ah, heaven, more!" she answered. "Mademoiselle is but a child; she does not know the delight of the feel, the soft lovely feel, of this that drapes so perfectly. Fortunately Mademoiselle lends herself to the lovely things. They become her. They cling to her figure as though they loved it. The result will be charming. M. le Capitaine Theobald he should be here to see the result. How his eyes would sparkle!"

"M. le Capitaine Theobald, as you call him, Louise," I said, "would not know one stuff from another. It is quite possible that he would like me better in the pink print yonder. The beautiful things will be quite wasted on him. He thinks a white muslin frock with a blue sash the finest thing a girl can wear."

"It is not bad, for an ingénue," said Louise, thoughtfully. "But I do not agree with you, Mademoiselle, that he would not admire these lovely things. He might not know, but he would admire all the same."

"Possibly," I said, with patience. I was not greatly interested in Theobald's point of view. I might have altered in my cousin's eyes; but he had hardly altered to me from the boy with whom I went climbing and skating in the old days. I could not imagine myself having any sentimentality about Theobald.

"Mademoiselle is too sensible for her years," said Louise; and I was conscious of a subtle disparagement in the speech.

"I am not sensible at all, Louise," I answered, with some indignation. "I am not sensible where grandpapa is concerned, nor grandmamma, I tremble if grandpapa is a little later on a hunting day than we expect him, or on Wednesday when the petty sessions are on at Quinn. I am terrified about grandmamma if her finger aches; and I lie awake at night imagining all the terrible things that could befall them."

"Ah, that is affectionateness. I never said you were not affectionate, Mademoiselle."

But there was some meaning in Louise's accusation, although she would say no more, pretending that she was always one to let her tongue run away with her. Louise had been with Miss Champion these twenty years, and was a privileged person as old servants are amongst us.

When she had finished I went to look for my godmother, and found her with Miss Standish, bathing her forehead with eau-de-Cologne.

"Poor little Bawn," she said, "you look tired. Louise has kept you standing too long. Once set Louise to fitting clothes and she forgets everything. Could you not sit down here and rest a while before starting for home?"

"Yes, why not sit with me for a while?" Miss Standish put in eagerly. "I always find your voice restful, Bawn."

But I would not stay. I had promised my grandmother to be home by half-past six at latest, and I was not going to have her fretting about my absence. It was six o'clock now and the shadows were growing longer; the coolness of evening was coming. The birds were singing their even-song. As I went down the marble steps in the grassy terraces from the house I saw the peacock and his lady already at roost in a low tree, although the darkness would not come for some hours yet, and indeed would be then only a green twilight.

There was never anything to be afraid of on our roads. Our valley was in such a quiet isolation, so far away from the main roads, that even a tramp or an importunate beggar were not to be feared. The labourers going home from the fields touched their caps with a friendly "God save you kindly, Miss Bawn." The children by the cottage doors smiled at me shyly. Even the dogs knew me. It was the road I had taken to the Creamery and back every day; and I had been familiar with it from my childhood.

The sun was yet so hot on the exposed road that Dido and I were glad to get within the shelter of Daly's Wood. Though the sun poured upon the wood it was cool within it and steeped in a golden haze. The pale stems of the springing trees looked like so many great candles in a golden house; there was a sweet sound of falling waters, for a little mountain stream ran through the wood, and in its neighbourhood the air was damp and deliciously sweet. Where the water tumbled over broken boulders and formed a little pool Dido stood to drink, and I stood, too, a minute listening to the bird-songs of which the wood was full.

When we had turned round and gone on our way I observed that there was some one sitting on the stile which led out on the road nearly opposite the postern gate in our park wall and supposed it to be someone resting there who would rise up to let me pass.

I could not imagine myself being afraid of these quiet places, where, no matter what happened elsewhere, the people were always friendly and respectful. But as I came close up to the man who sat on the stile and who had not turned his head at the sound of my foot on the path, all of a sudden I became filled with a nameless terror.

The wide shoulders, the rather massive head with the closely curling red hair; I seemed to recognize them all at once for Richard Dawson's, and I was as frightened as ever was a hare of the dogs; nay, more frightened, for the hare has at least her speed. My feet seemed clogged by leaden weights as they might be in the terror of a dream. Then the man turned about with a smile which showed all his white teeth and I was sick with fear.

"It is the third day I have been waiting for you, you pretty creature," he said. "I am going to lift you over the stile, and then you shall give me a kiss for it."

He flung his arms about me and I closed my eyes while I tried to push him away. I felt his breath on my face, and my loathing of him was so great that it made me physically incapable of resistance. I uttered one cry, but I felt that there was no body of sound in it to carry it even if anybody had been near. But suddenly I heard a furious growl, and I felt myself released.

"Damn the brute! She has bitten me," he said furiously.

And there he was with the blood running down his hand, while my brave old dog stood by ready to defend me against all the world.

CHAPTER IX

A ROUGH LOVER

For a second or two we stood staring at each other while Richard Dawson mopped the blood from his hand.

"Don't you see that your damned dog has bitten me?" he shouted, as though my silence infuriated him.

"I see," I said with my hand on Dido's collar to restrain her. "You shouldn't have been rude to me, sir."

He stopped staunching his wound and burst into a great roar of laughter which had no good humour in it.

"Lord, lord!" he said. "That's the best thing I've heard of this many a day. Why a little country hussy like you ought to be honoured by receiving a gentleman's kisses. There, my dear, get rid of your dog. I don't want to kick her brains out as I could easily do, and as she deserves to have done for having bitten me. Send her home with a stone at her heels and come and sit by me on the stile. You shall see how prettily a gentleman makes love."

I suppose I must have looked at him with the horror I felt for him, for he laughed again.

"What," he said, "am I so ugly as all that? I can tell you, my dear, that a good many of your sex, both small and great, regard me as a very pretty fellow. In fact, I'm pestered with the women. I assure you I really am, my dear. And so you won't give me a kiss of your own free will? Why, I could take it if I liked; but I'm not sure that I want to take it till you come and offer it to me of your own free will."

"That I shall never do," I said.

"I'm not so sure of that," he replied. "There aren't many ladies in this county wouldn't give me a kiss if I wanted it, much less a little dairymaid like you."

I thought at the time that it was his egregious vanity and conceit, but in this I was wrong, as events afterwards proved. Indeed, it was a very strange thing how women, both gentle and simple, were in many cases attracted by the coarse good looks and insolent, swaggering way of Richard Dawson, an inconceivable thing to me in the case of a lady, although more easily understood in the case of a poor peasant girl like Nora Brady.

His mood had apparently changed, and I was less afraid of him, although my detestation of him had been deepened by his conduct to me.

He still sat on the stile so that I could not pass him; but all the anger had gone out of his face, although the blood still trickled a little from the back of his hand where Dido had planted her teeth.

"Will you let me pass, please?" said I.

"Presently, my dear." How I hated him for his easy insolence! "I want to hear first what it is you dislike in me."

"Everything," I answered.

"Why," he said mockingly, "it is a thing of spirit, and it will be the more pleasure to tame it. I am tired of birds that come fluttering into my hands and cling to me when I no longer desire them. Upon my word, I like you the better for it. Come, I'm sorry I frightened you. I can say no more than that; it is the fault of your sex, which is so complaisant."

He put his hand into his pocket and drew out a handful of coins.

"Here's a sovereign," he said, "to buy a ribbon. It can't make you prettier, but may it make you kinder when next we meet!"

He flung the coin as though he expected me to catch it, but, of course, I made no effort to do so and it fell on the ground and rolled away into a heap of dead leaves. No matter what happened I could not have kept myself from kicking at it contemptuously with my foot where it lay.

"Not enough, eh?" he asked, his eyebrows raised in amusement. "Would five do?"

I stared at him and the colour flamed in my cheeks.

"Why, you are prettier than ever," he said. "If you look at me like that much longer I shall be obliged to kiss you, although I would rather wait till you came offering me a kiss. Pretty spitfire! Where have they been hiding you? I had no idea, till I saw you the other day at the Creamery, that there was anything so pretty hereabouts. I generally find out what there is delectable in the way of femininity before I am forty-eight hours in a place. You have no idea of what an adorable little modesty you looked with your white arms plunged in the milk. You took the shine out of the ladies, my dear."

I could only look at him with steady animosity, while my hand on her collar kept poor Dido in check. I saw that he took me for a peasant girl and I was not minded to enlighten him. I was going away; and perhaps before I came back he would be gone again on his travels, for I had always heard that he was wild and a rover and could not be persuaded to settle down and live at Damerstown although his father and mother were most anxious that he should. My heartfelt desire at the moment was that I should never again see Richard Dawson's face, with its insolent and coarse good looks, as long as I lived.

"Yes, you took the shine out of the fine ladies that were with me that day," he went on, "fine a conceit as they have of themselves. They were fine London ladies, my dear, the sort that play cards all night, and motor all day, and have no time to be God-fearing and loving like the women that went before them. You didn't look at them?"

The speech struck me as oddly incongruous in parts of it, yet we had heard—about the one thing we had heard in his favour—that he was fond of his old mother, a good-natured, homely, kindly body, people said, who was rather unhappy among the Dawson riches, rather afraid of her granite-faced, beetling-browed husband.

"No, I didn't look at them," I said.

"And why not, pray?"

"I took no interest in them. I did not like their way of speaking. They seemed vulgar to me."

I hardly knew why I answered him. Perhaps he compelled me. When I had answered he turned round and looked at me with an uproarious delight in his face.

"If Lady Meg could only hear you! Lord! lord!" he said, with infinite gusto. "The daughter of a hundred earls! And Miss Moxon, just as high born and just as fast! How amazed they would be. They would box your pretty ears, my dear; at least Lady Meg would."

"That they would not," I answered him. "And now, please let me pass."

"Without a kiss?" he said mockingly. "Very well, then, I shall let you go. But I feel myself a poor-spirited fellow for it. Do you know that your eyes are like wet violets? And when do we meet again, my dear?"

However, though he mocked he stood aside to let me pass, which at first I hesitated to do, fearing that he might perhaps seize me in his arms as I passed him.

To my great vexation he seemed to guess at this feeling of mine, for he laughed again and said—

"Don't be afraid, pretty one. I promised to let you pass and I shall. No one shall say that Dick Dawson's word isn't as good as his bond; and his bond is worth a good deal. He ought to know something of bonds too, seeing the way the money was made."

So he mocked at himself when he was not mocking at me. I did not altogether trust him, but I made up my mind that if he was rude to me again my poor dog should protect me as she had done before. But after all there was no necessity, for with a sudden movement my enemy lifted his hat, turned away and walked down the road, smiling at me, as he went, over his shoulder.

Never was any one so glad of a place of refuge as I was when I went in at the postern gate in the wall and was within our own woods. I tried to shoot the rusty bolt into its place, but it had been unused for years and I could not move it, so I let it be. And now it was twilight in the dark woods but I felt at home, and letting Dido go, she bounded on before me as though she were young again, and I followed more sedately, with an occasional glance back to see I was not followed.

CHAPTER X

THE TRAP

The sight of the red sun sinking down a long, green avenue turned my thoughts for a moment from the painful memory of Richard Dawson's rudeness, which, now that I had escaped from him, made me feel sick and ashamed.

It was something I could never tell to anybody, and I felt as though I must carry some shameful secret all my days and that it must appear in my face, and I was glad that I need not meet the eyes of my grandparents by daylight, but could deceive their dear, dim sight in the shaded candle-light and afterwards have the night to recover myself.

With a young girl's extremity of virginal pride and modesty, I hated even myself because he had touched me and could have disfigured the face he had praised.

But the red sun glinting down the long arcades, promising another fine day to-morrow, gave my thoughts a welcome turn. I remembered how it had shone yesterday in the long line of windows at Brosna; and that led me to think of Anthony Cardew.

He had the most romantic stories attaching to him, such stories as were sure to please a young girl's fancy. It was to be sure not a name we mentioned at Aghadoe. Indeed, even before I knew about Uncle Luke there was something that forbade my talking of the Cardews before Lord and Lady St. Leger or before my godmother.

Only old Maureen, who so often mixed up the present and the past, would talk of the Cardews as though their name had never been banned, as though they still came and went as friends and intimates at Aghadoe Abbey as in the days before the trouble came about Uncle Luke.

I knew that Captain Cardew had long since retired from the army, and that one never knew in what corner of the world he might not be, since wherever adventures were to be found he was.

I knew that he had spent many years of his life—he must be now nearly forty, which was a great age to me—in the service of an unhappy great lady whose little kingdom had been unjustly taken from her, and in her cause he had spent his patrimony which had once been great. And now since she no longer lived, having given up her gentle soul some two years after she had sought the shelter of the convent against a rough world, he was free once more to devote his sword of Don Quixote to some other lost cause.

I knew, furthermore, that he was reported to have raised money from Mr. Dawson of Damerstown at ruinous interest to spend it in the service of the Princess Pauline, and that he was now very poor, too poor to keep his old home from going to pieces and being consumed by the damp and by rats and mice and general decay.

People used to wonder he did not try to sell it. Indeed, it was common talk that before Mr. Dawson had bought Damerstown he had tried to obtain possession of Brosna, and that his offer had been refused by Anthony Cardew with contempt. The common talk even found words for the refusal.

"What?" Captain Cardew was reported to have said. "You have plucked me clean enough, God knows, but I keep my honour intact, and that forbids that I should see Dawsons in the house where Cardews lived honourably and wronged none but themselves."

The low sun going down in a blaze behind the trees brought these things into my mind. I remember that the wood was as sweet from the scent of the white-thorn and the lilacs and a thousand other sweet and fresh things as though some heavenly censer swung there. The thrushes and the blackbirds were singing their wildest as is their custom about sunset; and below their triumphant songs you could hear the whole chorus of the little birds' voices as well as the fiddling and harping of the myriad field-crickets and grasshoppers. Then from the field beyond the wood I could hear the corncrakes sawing away in the yet unmown grass, and there were a great many wood-doves uttering their soft laments.

I have always loved the things of nature; but on this evening they had less power than usual to soothe me. The shame of my recent encounter with Richard Dawson kept sending the colour to my cheeks and the little shocks of repulsion through my blood. I felt that if he had really kissed me I must have killed him or myself. My fingers twitched as I thought on a certain dagger, little but deadly, which lay in a glass case in the picture-gallery, and I resolved that I would carry it in my breast for the future on my country rambles lest I should meet again with such rudeness as I had met to-day and have nothing with which to defend myself.

I was so engaged in my thoughts as I walked along that I had not noticed how far ahead of me Dido had run. But suddenly she was brought to my mind by the most horrible yelping which made me run as fast as ever I ran in my life.

I came up with her in a little glade away from the main path, a mere gamekeepers' passage, now much overgrown and choked up, for it was long since we had kept gamekeepers. I had to creep on my hands and knees through the briars and undergrowth to reach the place where she was, which was a clear space in the midst of the tangle.

As soon as she saw me she left off yelping and waited for me with an air of expectancy, as though she knew that I would soon put an end to her discomfort.

But alas for the poor thing's faith in me, I saw when I came up to her that her foot was caught in a trap, a horrible iron-toothed thing, the like of which I had never seen before. It must have rusted there from the old days till my poor dog by some accident had released it. I saw that there were bones by it—the bones of some poor wild creature, doubtless, who had perished in it, and the bones had no doubt acted as a warning to the others.

As I knelt down Dido licked my face frantically, being quite sure I was going to release her. But that was not so easy. Pull as I would I could not bring the teeth of the trap apart.

"I shall have to go for help, Dido," I said, after a few minutes, trusting to her sense to understand. But as I rose to go and she saw that I was leaving her, she began immediately a loud, almost hysterical barking, interspersed with little piteous moans and whimpers which were most painful to hear.

I did not know what to do, so I began to cry myself, and then I knelt down beside her and began again my useless effort to release her.

The sun by now was sinking low, although there would be light for an hour or two yet. I guessed that it must be seven o'clock, and I knew that my grandmother would be uneasy about me, and that presently my grandfather would have to be told, and the whole household would be anxious. What was I to do? I could not even think that they would come this way looking for me, since they had not known of my intention of coming home by Daly's Wood and the postern.

I was in the greatest perplexity and distress, and I never was so glad in my life as when I heard a shout close at hand. I believe that if it had been Richard Dawson himself I should have welcomed him at that moment.

"Come this way, please," I called out. "My dog is caught in a trap and I cannot leave her."

I heard someone come as I had come, on hands and knees, through the undergrowth; then he emerged into the little glade and stood upright, the grass and the leaves about his clothing.

He did not look at me at first, but came, with that clucking of the tongue against the palate which we use in Ireland as a sound of pity and concern, to the rescue of the dog. His hands, fine and long and slender, tore the trap apart as though it had been paper.

"Poor beast!" he said, "she is very little the worse. The teeth of the trap had grown blunt, although they were strong enough to hold her."

I thought him the very finest gentleman I had ever seen or ever hoped to see, and that is to say a good deal, since it would not be easy to find a finer gentleman than my grandfather. And I had the portrait of Uncle Luke and my childish memory of him. And Theobald is as fine and gallant a young gentleman as you would wish to see.

But this stranger was finer than any of them.

Suddenly he looked at me for the first time, and I saw his face change. Some wave of emotion passed over it, troubling its gay serenity. His lips trembled. And then he was himself again.

"Pardon me," he said. "For the moment I thought I had seen a ghost—as though ghosts apparelled themselves like the rose! You are very like someone I once knew who is now dead. I am so glad I have been able to help your poor dog."

I stammered like the rustic Richard Dawson had taken me for. Who could this finest of fine gentlemen be?

CHAPTER XI

THE FRIEND

He was tall and slim, and had an elegance of air which really does not seem to belong to our age. His face was bronzed and his eyes were of so dark a grey—I know since that they are grey—that I thought them black that evening in the shadow of the woods.

He had a little black moustache, and, in odd contrast to it and his look of youth, his hair was quite white. It was perhaps that which gave him his air of elegance. He was really like a powdered gallant of the last century rather than a gentleman of this. But his speech was of this, and very Irish as well.

"I am so glad I was able to assist you," he said. "There, good dog, good dog!" to Dido, who was fawning upon him. "Let me see! She goes a little lame, but there is no harm done. She will be quite well in a day or two. And this shall do no further damage."

I suppose it was no great thing, seeing that the trap was old and rusty, but it seemed to me a great feat of strength when his long fingers tore it apart and flung the two halves into the bushes.

"They are murderous things," he said. "Every man who laid one should himself be caught in it."

"I am grateful to you forever," I said. "What would I have done if you had not been at hand? I could not leave Dido. If I had she would have broken her leg in the effort to escape. And try as I would, I could not force the trap apart."

"To be sure not," he said, glancing at my hands; "and I'm very glad I came by. By the way, I was trespassing, I'm afraid. If Lord St. Leger or any of his family had come upon me I should have been ordered out of the woods."

"Oh no," I said, with some indignation. "That you would not have been. I am Bawn Devereux, Lord St. Leger's granddaughter. We are not so churlish."

He lifted his hat again.

"Lord St. Leger's popularity is well known," he said. "It has always been a friendly and generous race. Yet I think I should have been turned out of the woods."

"Do not say so," I implored him, in a passion of vexation. "My grandfather would love you because of what you have done for the dog. He is devoted to dumb animals. In any case, he would not have objected to a gentleman walking in his woods. That the postern gate is left open is a proof that people come and go as they will."

"That may be," he said. "The St. Legers have always been at peace with their fellow-men, yet I would not be caught a trespasser."

There was a sudden darkness by which I conjectured that the sun had sunk below the horizon.

"I must be going," I said in a great hurry. "They will be anxious about me at home. For the rest, I give you the freedom of the woods. Come and go when you will. You are welcome to Aghadoe."

His face lit up.

"Faith, it's pleasant to a homeless man like myself to be assured of a welcome," he said. "And now, Miss Bawn, let me see you to the confines of the wood, within sight of the Abbey. Out on the hills and plains it is yet day, but in the woods night comes early, to give a chance perhaps to the birds who have been awake since cock-crow."

I crept out of the glade as I had entered it and he followed me. When we both stood upright in the wood-path we laughed together.

"I believe I knew the place of old," he said, "when I was a little urchin. Sure there's no place like home, after all."

I had been wondering who he might be, and had fancied he was a visitor at one of the houses of the neighbourhood, perhaps at the Ardaraghs', but his speech showed me that he must belong to the county.

"My grandfather would like to thank you," I said, as we walked along the wood-path, where I was glad of his company. Now that the shades closed in, and with the postern gate open, how could I tell that Richard Dawson might not lie in wait for me? He had thought me a peasant girl, the wretch, and offered me money for my kisses. The wave of resentment and disgust in my mind swelled to the full. This gentleman who walked beside me had known me for a lady despite my print frock. I was furious for the moment with Lady Ardaragh and the others who would admit such people as the Dawsons to their drawing-rooms, and I was proud to think that Aghadoe Abbey shut its doors against mere money. There were few things we thought less of than money at Aghadoe.

"Lord St. Leger would like to thank you," I said. "Will you not come in and see him?"

"Why, no," he answered, "although I am loth to say no to so gracious an invitation. Believe me, I am not insensible of the graciousness that prompts it. Ah, here we are in sight of the Abbey. I shall stand and watch till I see you safe within its doors."

While we were yet in the obscurity of the wood he lifted my hand to his lips.

"I am eternally grateful to the good fortune that gave me the chance of serving you," he said.

"I wish you would come and be thanked," I answered in a low voice. I had the oddest reluctance to leave him, with no prospect of ever seeing him again.

"Who knows but we may meet again?" he answered, yet did not offer to tell his name, and I felt shy of asking it.

I turned back on the doorstep when I had come to it, and saw across the lawn and shrubbery his shadowy shape standing at the edge of the wood. I waved my hand to him and he lifted his hat. The sun looked out for the last time from under a purple cloud and I saw him plainly. While I gazed towards him the darkness came again and I lost him; and there was Neil Doherty, our butler, opening the door to me and upbraiding me as he had done when I was a small child.

"Musha, where have you been stravaigin' to, Miss Bawn? and her Ladyship in and out like a dog at a fair, axin', 'Is Miss Bawn in yet, Neil?' His Lordship doesn't know, glory be, or maybe 'tis havin' a bad attack of the gout he'd be. If I was you, Miss Bawn, I'd give up the Creamery, so I would, or lave it to the commonalty! Sure 'twould be fitter for the like o' you to be sittin' at home in the drawing-room, playin' the piano-forty. Yes, your Ladyship, here she is at last. I was just tellin' her that your Ladyship was like a hen on a hot griddle waitin' for her."

"Dear child, you are late," my grandmother said, breaking in on Neil's eloquence, which indeed generally had to be interrupted, for once Neil started there was no knowing when he would leave off.

"It was Dido," I said, telling half the truth. Not for worlds could I have told my grandmother of how Richard Dawson had insulted me. "It was Dido, who caught her foot in a trap. It was an old rusty trap. I do not know how long it can have been there. But it held Dido fast, and she would not let me leave her. I should have been there still if it had not been for the timely help of a gentleman who was passing through the wood and heard her yelping. She made enough noise to wake the dead."

"Ah, poor Dido!"

My grandmother's attention was diverted to the dog, who was especially dear to her for Uncle Luke's sake. She sat down now in the great hooded chair which was supposed to belong to Neil Doherty, only that he did so many things in the house that he never had much time for sitting in state in the hall. She took Dido's paws in her lap and began anxiously to examine them for any injury, while the dog moaned with self-pity.

"I don't think she has any hurt," I assured her. "The trap did not altogether meet on her paw, although it held her a prisoner."

Neil Doherty looked on with an interested face.

"Twould be a kindness to the poor baste," he said, "to drown her, not to be keepin' her alive. Sure, what has she to live for?"

My grandmother looked up at him with a sudden illumination of her face.

"Who knows, Neil," she said, "but Dido may have something to live for yet? And that the thing others of us are living for?"

"Ah, sure you're right, your Ladyship," Neil returned. "Sure God send it! Wouldn't we be all young again if that was to happen?"

CHAPTER XII

THE ENEMY

My grandmother asked me no more of the gentleman who had come to my help in the wood. Being old she forgot easily, and, besides, she was absorbed in these days in the preparations for my going to Dublin.

For the moment my own interest in the great matter had waned. I used to like to slip away from the perpetual fitting on of garments to ride or drive about the roads outside the Abbey. I was afraid now to walk in unfrequented places, lest I should meet with Richard Dawson; and there are few places in the neighbourhood of Aghadoe which are frequented. I grew quite zealous about afternoon calls, and would remind my grandmother of her neglect of her social duties, a matter which had never troubled me before.

"Why, what has come to you, Bawn?" she asked at length. "You have always been unwilling to make calls before, from the time you were a little girl of six, and I thought it would be a fine thing to take you and Theobald in the barouche to call on Mrs. Langdale, but when I looked for you I could find you nowhere and afterwards I discovered that you had both hidden in the loft in the stable-yard. Well, I suppose you are growing up and this is a sign of it."

I did not undeceive her. I had always abhorred the afternoon calls and the dinner-parties, and most of the other social functions to which I had gone; but now it was another matter. To be sure, when I made my calls I had always the dread of meeting Richard Dawson; but then on the other hand there was always the chance that I might meet that other.

Although he had told me nothing it was certain that he must be staying at some of the houses of the neighbourhood. All I wonder at was that I heard nothing of him when I made my various calls, for even very slight matters, very unimportant and uninteresting persons, are the subject of much discussion in our drawing-rooms, since we see so little of the outside world. And he was not unimportant, not uninteresting. I should have thought they would have talked of nothing else.

My grandmother was very busy in these days. All the old friendships which she had let slip were to be taken up again for me. She spent much time at her desk, and the postbag for the Abbey began to contain many delicate, fragrant epistles.

"I am only sorry, Bawn," she said, looking up at me over her shoulder as I stood behind her chair, "that we cannot open the town-house for you and give a ball for you there. It is what ought to be done, but, of course, it is out of the question. But you must go and see the house, child. It has glorious memories. It is very much impoverished now, and it will be all in dust and darkness; but there the best blood and brains, aye, and hearts of Ireland, used to come. There came Grattan, and Burke, and Flood, and Lord Charlemont. And there came poor Pamela Fitzgerald and her Edward. All that was beautiful and witty in the Ireland of those days moved through the rooms which you will find dark and dusty."

She broke off for a moment and looked straight before her, as though she saw visions, and when she looked up at me again her dear eyes were dim.

"If things had been otherwise," she went on, "we need not have shut up the house, with only Maureen's sister, Bridget, to look after it. Still, Mary Champion will see to your enjoyment, Bawn; and I am surprised to find how many people yet remember me in Dublin. You are sure of a hearty welcome for your grandfather's sake and mine from the old friends. You will make your own way with the young. But now, since I have letters to write, Bawn, and they must be long ones, supposing you go yourself this afternoon and call on Lady Ardaragh and the Chenevixes. You can have the phaeton and drive yourself. And you can leave cards for me. My card-case is on the table."

Now, I thought it quite possible that he might be a guest of the Ardaraghs, who had always people staying with them. On the other hand, it was a house where I always dreaded to meet Richard Dawson, for I had heard Lady Ardaragh say, when the Dawsons were coming to Damerstown and we were all full of indignation against them, that she for her part was delighted to hear of somebody who had money and that she for one would welcome the Dawsons.

"I think money the one good and desirable thing of all the world," she had said.

I remember that Sir Arthur, who was present, looked at her in some surprise, and that she repeated the speech with greater emphasis and a heightened colour. And afterwards my grandmother spoke of her with a certain pitying tenderness, saying to Mary Champion that she was too pretty and too young to be left so much to her own devices. I overheard the speech by accident, being in the oriel of the library where long ago I had heard my grandmother's speech to my grandfather concerning me. My grandmother was fond of Lady Ardaragh and so was I.

I had taken Mickey, my foster-brother who is devoted to me, to hold the pony when I should alight. Perhaps, also, out of fear that I might meet with Richard Dawson, alone and unprotected.

When we drove up in front of the Ardaraghs' house the hall door stood open. There was not a soul in sight; not even a friendly dog came down the steps to greet us, though usually there were half a dozen of them.

I rang and knocked but no one came. It was five in the afternoon, and I guessed that Lady Ardaragh might be out and the servants at tea somewhere in the back premises.

However, I was not to be put off by an unanswered bell since the door stood open. I knew my way about the house well, and was on terms of sufficient intimacy to announce myself.

I guessed that the most likely place to find Lady Ardaragh would be the little inner drawing-room of which she had made a boudoir, to which were admitted only her favoured and intimate visitors.

I went through the house without meeting any one. There was not a sound. Often at this hour Lady Ardaragh had the boy with her; but if he had been there now I should have heard his shouts and laughter as I had heard them before. However cold and strange she might be to her serious husband Lady Ardaragh was a lovely mother, and she never looked to greater advantage than when she was romping with her boy down on the floor, her beautiful hair pulled about her, flushed, happy, smiling, as I have seen her.

No, certainly the child was not there now. As I crossed the large drawing-room I began to think there was no one there. The pale yellow silk curtains that screened the arch by which one entered the inner room were drawn close. Just outside them I paused for a second; I had almost turned back; then I heard a low laugh and there was the pleasant tinkle of teacups.

I raised the curtain to pass through, and found beyond it a French screen. I was about to pass around it into the room when I glanced up at the wall, on which hung an old-fashioned convex mirror. It reflected the room and its occupants with a minute delicacy. Her Ladyship, more like a Dresden-china figure than ever in a teagown of flowered silk, lolled in a low chair. She was holding a teacup in her pretty beringed hands. In the mirror her colour seemed more than usually high. She was very gay, animated and smiling.

There was a man with her. His back was to the mirror and at first I did not notice him. He was sitting on a tabouret, which must have been an uncomfortable seat for one of his height and length of limb. He had an air of sitting at Lady Ardaragh's feet.

I had an idea that my presence would be an intrusion, even before the man in the mirror turned his head and I recognized him.

My heart gave a great leap. Fortunately they were talking and had not heard me. Once beyond the curtain I fled as fast as my two feet would carry me back to Mickey and the phaeton.

CHAPTER XIII

ENLIGHTENMENT

The man I had seen was Richard Dawson, and I had not even known that Lady Ardaragh knew him, although I had suspected that she would know him in time. And here he was on terms of such easy intimacy as the scene I had come upon implied. I had been fond of Sybil Ardaragh, but for the moment I felt cold and angry towards her. It was a degradation that she should be friends, should flirt, with a man like Richard Dawson. What was she thinking of, the mother of Robin, the wife of Sir Arthur Ardaragh, who was a person of great wisdom and dignity, with a fame beyond our quiet circles? It was not worthy of her.

We went on and called at Rosebower, the little house of the two Miss Chenevixes, elderly ladies who had been great beauties in their youth. I used to think they were beauties still, with their fine, delicate features and skin no more withered than a rose of yesterday.

Miss Bride was classical, like a Muse, with her dark silky hair just streaked with grey, looped away behind her ears; while Miss Henrietta, the younger, had ringlets and large eyes and a languishing air.

It was enough for them to hear that I was going to Dublin for there to be quite a commotion. The one little maid brought in the tea, which Miss Bride poured out of a china pot into little teacups which were all of different colours, although of the same design. The tea was fragrant and strong, with thick cream in it; and when I begged for a little water to be added the two sisters broke out in protestations. That would be a real slur on their hospitality, and, seeing how they took it to heart, I was obliged to set my own liking aside and drink the tea as it was.

There were slices of thin bread and butter and sandwiches and toast under a silver cover, all of which I could have eaten myself, for I had an excellent appetite. But I denied myself again, and was rewarded by hearing Miss Henrietta declare, on her second scrap of bread and butter, that she had a most indelicate appetite, and she hoped her dear young friend, meaning me, would not be shocked at her.

I could always spend an hour or two happily in the little low-browed cottage drawing-room, with even the strong May light coming in greenly, having been filtered through the new leaves. It was a room that always pleased my imagination, for it was so full of bits of china and pictures, of old silver and ivory curios and nicknacks, that you could spend a day looking at them. On the low walls were several portraits of pretty ladies, to whom the Misses Chenevix bore the strongest resemblance. Because there had been rain earlier in the day there was a fire in the grate and the firelight sparkled prettily on the glass of the pictures, on the china and silver, and in the brooches and rings of the ladies.

A half-glass door led from the drawing-room into an old-fashioned garden which was now nearing the last of its bloom, and presently would show a most wonderful profusion of fruit; giant strawberries, currants like strings of carbuncles and rubies, raspberries larger and juicier than mulberries, with a great quantity of apples and pears and plums and apricots to follow.

The sun had come out after the rain, and I could see from where I sat the garden sparkling; and the box borders smelt very sweet.

Both the ladies were eager to know what clothes I was to have and to learn what friends I was going to see and what festivities I should attend; and Miss Bride took care to impress upon me that my visit was to be paid at a hopelessly unfashionable time of year.

"There'll be nothing doing at the Castle," she said. "I wouldn't be bothered going to Dublin unless I was to dine at the Castle."

"I dare say Bawn will find plenty of other entertainment, sister, even though she does not visit at the Castle," Miss Henrietta put in; she was always the conciliatory one. "There will be plenty of people in Dublin," she went on, "who will be very glad to see Bawn—old friends of Lady St. Leger and of Mary Champion."

"Did I say it was quite empty?" Miss Bride asked, with some asperity. "To be sure, there are always people. But she'll miss the best of it. She ought to be there for the Patrick's Ball and the command nights at the theatre. The last time I was at the Theatre Royal I was in the Viceregal box. She was a sweet, pretty creature, and His Excellency had a beautifully turned leg. We drove to Punchestown with them the following day. I remember the hundreds and hundreds of jaunting-cars tearing like mad along the road. To be sure we had outriders, but it was nearly as much as your life was worth, and coming out at the Gap afterwards we had a horse's hind legs in our carriage, and every one screaming like mad, and the dust fit to choke you. Even motors couldn't rival that."

She spoke with an air of grave exhilaration. They knew everybody and everything that was fine and gay in the social life of their day. Perhaps they would know about my fine gentleman. I only hesitated to ask because in her latter years Miss Bride had adopted a manner of hostility towards the male sex generally, and was apt to snap at any one who showed an interest in it even of the slightest. However, I screwed up my courage.

"Miss Chenevix," I began, "I met a gentleman the other day in our wood and I wondered who he might be. I can't imagine where he was staying. And I thought I would ask you if you knew who he was."

"We could do very well without men," Miss Bride said sharply. "In fact, the world could have got on very well without them. There is nothing a man can do that a woman can not do better. What was your gentleman like, Bawn?"

Despite her hostility to the male sex Miss Bride was very curious.

"He was very slim and elegant," I began—"not very young."

"Now what do you mean by not very young, Bawn? Be precise in your statements," Miss Bride said, with some asperity.

"I should say he was quite forty," I said, blushing, and wishing I had not mentioned the matter of age."

"Fiddlesticks, child! Forty is young. And so you met this young gentleman in the wood. And what happened?"

"He took Dido's paw out of a trap. He was very kind about it," I returned, conscious of Miss Bride's severe eye.

"There was no philandering, child, now was there? You're not long out of short frocks. I can't imagine how the young gentleman came to be in your woods. You'd better forget all about him, but first tell me what he was like and all that happened."

"Bride! The poor child!" said Miss Henrietta, compassionately.

"There was no philandering," I said composedly. I am used to Miss Chenevix's ways. "How could there be? He rendered me such a service as any gentleman might have done, and went on his way. It was only seeing that we have so few strangers—"

"He might be staying at Damerstown. They have a houseful."

"I am sure he was not."

"Hoity-toity! how can you know if you know nothing about him? Tell me again what he was like. I know everyone who goes in and out of every house in the county except Damerstown, and there are too many of them for me, besides which old Dawson ruined my uncle Hercules. Was he tall? You say he was tall."

"Tall and slight."

"Regular features?"

"A straight nose; his face clean shaven except for a small dark moustache; a good deal of colour in his face and great vivacity."

"And his eyes? There, you needn't tell me. I ought to know. The eyes are grey with dark lashes. You might take them for black. It is Anthony Cardew to the life."

"Snow-white hair," I added.

"Snow-white hair," Miss Bride repeated. "No, no. It can't be Anthony Cardew, unless there are white blackbirds. Hair black as jet."

"Perhaps Captain Cardew may have become white, sister," Miss Henrietta put in humbly.

"White! What would make him white?" Miss Bride asked angrily. "He can't be forty. I remember him the very day his sister was run away with—"

She pulled herself up suddenly, and turned to me with an air of great kindness.

"'Tis my tongue is running away with me," she said. "Excuse me, Bawn, my dear. Your stranger sounds like Anthony Cardew, but I don't see that it can be he. He was raven-black. Better think no more of him. I wouldn't waste a thought on any man. I wonder why the Lord made them."

I had stood up to go. I think I had known all the time that my fine gentleman and Anthony Cardew were one and the same, had understood all the time why he was so certain that his presence in our woods would be unwelcome to my grandparents.

"You never know where he might be, Anthony Cardew," Miss Bride went on, holding my hand. "One day at one end of Europe, the next at the other. Don't think of him, child. He is better worth thinking of than most men, but none of them are worth it. Good-bye, Bawn; be sure and write us word of all your fine doings."

Miss Henrietta came with me to the phaeton to whisper in my ear that I was not to mind her sister's odd views about gentlemen, because poor Bride lived in perpetual fear that she, Miss Henrietta, might marry and leave her.

CHAPTER XIV

THE MINIATURE

As we jogged along in the evening coolness and sweetness, we came upon Sir Arthur Ardaragh with little Robin on his shoulder. The boy shouted with joy when he saw me; and when I had stopped the phaeton he called down from his height about the picnic tea father and he had had in the fields, his little fat hand upon his father's neck while he told it.

"Robin often won't eat a good tea in the nursery," his father explained. "I think he wants other little boys to make him eat; he eats a famous tea when we have it together out-of-doors and travel a distance before we have it."

"I never want other boys, dada," Robin said, "when I have you. You are better than a brother even."

"Have you been to see Sybil?" Sir Arthur asked, recapturing the young gentleman and lifting him again to his shoulder.

To my annoyance, I felt my cheeks grow red, but his kind, serious eyes showed no knowledge of it. I wished they were not so far away, those eyes, so absorbed with books and dead and gone people and dead languages. I wished they were nearer home, took more obvious thought for the pretty young wife whom I had sometimes imagined to be jealous of her husband's absorption in his studies.

"I called, but I did not see Lady Ardaragh," I said.

"Ah, I suppose she had gone out. Well, good-bye, Miss Devereux. Remember me kindly to Lord and Lady St. Leger."

A day or two later I heard my godmother mention to Lady St. Leger, when I was not supposed to be listening, that someone had seen Anthony Cardew. He had passed a night at Brosna, and he was off somewhere to the South Seas, on some romantic, treasure-hunting expedition which he had been asked to join.

"Will he never settle down?" my grandmother asked in a whisper. I noticed that they always whispered when they mentioned the name of Cardew, on account of my grandfather, no doubt, for he would always have it that Irene Cardew had been the cause of the tragedy which had resulted in Jasper Tuite's death and Uncle Luke's exile, and he hated her and Brosna and all the Cardews on her account.

"He shows no sign of it," my godmother answered. "I have little cause to love the Cardews, but Anthony is a fine fellow. It is a thousand pities that his life must be sacrificed to the memory of a woman who was always beyond his reach, even while she lived."

Perhaps if they had talked more openly I should have been less interested in the Cardews; but the mystery which hung about Brosna and its owners for me had had the effect as I grew up of stimulating my curiosity about them. And now that I knew I did not feel called upon to hate them. Even if Irene Cardew had played fast and loose between Jasper Tuite and Uncle Luke there was no reason for hating her brother, who must have been but a boy at the time. I wondered if Irene had been like her brother Anthony, had worn in her delicacy the look of a rapier, a flame, of something bright and upstanding and alive with energy.

Since I might meet Richard Dawson and had no hope of meeting Anthony Cardew, I walked much those days within our own walls, which gave me space enough for Aghadoe park-walls are four miles in length.

But most often I found myself taking the path that led to the postern gate as though the place had some pleasant, dreamy association for me.

One day I had the whim to creep again within the little glade where Anthony Cardew had come to my help. It was now all hung about with wild roses and woodbine and was very sweet, and far overhead the trees met in a light, springing roof of green, more beautiful than any cathedral.

It had grown dark, and as I stood in the glade the rain pattered on the leaves overhead, but not a drop reached me. There were harebells and saxifrage in the moss, and underneath the bushes there was scented woodruff, and there was also sweet wild thyme. I thought I would make a summer drawing-room of the place, which none should know of beside myself, and should bring my books there and my needlework and embroidery, and spend long hours there alone or with a dog's companionship which is better than solitude.

The shower passed away over the hills, and the sun shone out. It sparkled here and there where a raindrop hung on a leaf and it suffused the glade with a warm, golden glow.

Suddenly something sparkled that was not a raindrop, something in the moss and undergrowth at the entrance to the glade. I wondered I had not seen it before, but it was the first time I had entered the glade since Anthony Cardew had been there.

I picked up the shining thing with great eagerness and found it to be a miniature set about with brilliants. My foot struck against something which proved to be a leather case in which the miniature, no doubt, had lain. As it fell the case must have opened, and that was a lucky thing, for if the miniature had remained in the case it might have lain there till the day of judgment. It was the mere accident of the stones sparkling that had caught my eye.

I stood with the miniature in my hand and stared at it, and it began to dawn upon me why Anthony Cardew had thought me a ghost. The face was far, far more beautiful than mine could ever be, yet it was strangely like the face that looked at me from the glass every morning when I did my hair.

To be sure, mine, I thought, was a poor simple, common face beside the face in the miniature with its wonderful expression. I have heard my grandmother say that the fair beauties of the South are the most beautiful of all, as beautiful as they are rare; and the original of the miniature had an opulent, golden beauty which we of the cold North could never attain. Perhaps the beauty might even have been over-opulent if sorrow and sadness had not given the face an air like a crowned martyr in heaven. So sweet it was, so gentle, so full of spiritual light, that I felt I could worship the owner of such a face.

Then I noticed the grand-ducal crown in diamonds at the top of the miniature, and it came to me that this was the portrait of the lady Anthony Cardew had served with a passionate devotion. No wonder I felt aflame for her, although I was only a girl; and I thought that so Mary Stuart must have looked to have left love of her alive in the world to this day.

I thought of how much the loss must have meant to Anthony Cardew, and cast wildly about in my mind for any means of letting him know that it was safe. But I could find none; and I could only hope that presently I should learn his whereabouts. I put the miniature into my breast for greater safety, and felt it warm there, as though a heart had been alive in it.

CHAPTER XV

THE EMPTY HOUSE

We had rooms on the sunny side of St. Stephen's Green, not far from the Shelbourne Hotel and the Clubs, and, what interested me more, the Grafton Street shops. I was nineteen years old, and I had never seen any shops but those of Quinn, our country town, and these very seldom; so it may be imagined what wonderful places the Dublin shops appeared to me, although my godmother assured me they were not a patch on those of London and Paris. In fact, the town seemed quite strange and wonderful altogether, with the people hurrying hither and thither and the traffic in the streets and the fine stir of life. I thought I never could be tired of it all; and I was quite sure I should never be tired of the shops.

My godmother was well pleased at my delight, while she laughed at me, assuring me that Dublin was a dead city as compared with others.

"It is a Sleeping Beauty which wakes once a year," she said, "and that is in Horse-Show Week. Time was when I came up every year for the show. Now I think I shall revive the custom for your sake, Bawn. We can bespeak these rooms if they are not already bespoken. I assure you, in Horse-Show Week, Bawn, people are glad to sleep anywhere. Even the bathrooms of houses and hotels are turned into bedrooms."

"I could not imagine a greater crowd than this," said I, for which she laughed at me, again calling me a country mouse.

Although the Castle season was over there was still a good deal going on, dinners and dances and many outdoor amusements, such as races and regattas and flower-shows, to many of which we went. And it was only when I saw how she enjoyed it all and how glad her old friends were to see her that I realized what a dull life she spent with us, always looking after that selfish invalid, her cousin, when she was not with old people like Lord and Lady St. Leger.

Also I realized, when I saw her in her fine gowns, what a stately, handsome woman she was still, and with an air of youth, although she had put away the things of youth from her.

Indeed, after the first, our lives seemed to me a whirl of gaiety, and although I went to no big balls, not having been presented, there were a good many young girls' dances and garden-parties and such things open to me, all of which I enjoyed greatly.

But one day, as it happened, my godmother was not very well, and our engagement for the afternoon had to be abandoned.

I remembered then that half our visit was over and I had not yet been to see Bridget Kelly, Maureen's sister, nor our old house which was in a sad and forsaken part of the city that hitherto we had not visited. I had had a great desire to see the old house all the time, but we had so many engagements. Now, when my godmother wanted sleep and darkness but was loth to leave me alone seemed to me an excellent moment.

"I shall go and see Bridget Kelly," I said, "while you rest. And when I come back you will be better."

"Not alone, Bawn?"

"You seem to forget I am twenty."

"But—a country mouse—and other things. I went about freely when I was your age, though the time was far more strict. But I could not let you walk about the city alone, child. Your grandmother would have a fit if she heard of such a thing."

At last I prevailed on her to let me go, on the understanding that I should take a cab which should wait to bring me back. I had a thousand times rather have had one of the outside cars, but I knew she would not hear of it unless she was with me, so I resigned myself to the stuffiness and rattling of a Dublin cab.

We crossed the city and climbed a steep hill and came presently to a region of darkness and desolation as it seemed to me, in which the houses were intolerably dreary—high, black houses that shut out the sky, fallen on evil days, since they were all sooty and grimy, with windows which had not been cleaned for years, many of them broken, and twisted and rusty railings guarding the areas.

I shuddered at the thought of the people who lived in such places.

I could see that they had once been places of consideration but now they were slums. Here and there a mean shop stood out, or the old house had been turned into a pawn office, or a builder's or baker's. Dirty children sat on the pavements or played in the gutters, while their dirty mothers gossiped in groups; and the men lounged to and from the public-houses, which were, indeed, the only bright spots in those dreadful streets.

I was relieved, when at last the cab stopped, that I had come to the end of my journey.

The last street down which we had driven was drearier than the rest, in a sense, but more respectable. There were wire blinds to all the lower windows, and there was no sign of life in the short street from end to end.

Our house crossed the end of the street, which was in a way an approach to it. It stood within stone walls, and was a great square building with wings thrown out, the style of it the pseudo-classical which was so much in favour in Ireland in the eighteenth century.

There was a great gate in the middle of the long wall; at one side of it a postern, which I pushed and found to be open. Bidding the driver wait for me I passed within.

I went up a flight of steps, under Ionic pillars, to the double hall door. I found that that, too, stood open, and I went into the hall, which was very dark despite the June sunshine without. It was an imposing hall paved with black and white marble, and the stairs ascending from it were of the same material. I was struck by the beautiful stucco work of the walls and ceiling. But dust and grime lay on everything and the air of the place struck cold.

I went back to the hall door and rang the bell, which echoed somewhere down in the lower regions of the house; but there was not a sound except that.

I rang again, and still no result, and the influence of the shut-up and abandoned house with all its shadows and memories began to chill me. I set the hall door open wide, and then I found the door at the back of the hall that led to the servants' quarters and opened that.

A rush of cold, damp air came up in my face with a mouldering smell.

"Bridget Kelly!" I called. "Bridget Kelly!"

The sound echoed as though through many vaults of stone and there was no answer.

The place and the silence began to get on my nerves. I remembered its forty-six rooms, all shut up and the furniture swathed in holland where the rooms were not empty. I have always had a dread of an empty house, and now it seized upon me. I could have run away out into the sunshine to the cabman whom I had left feeding his horse. When I had looked back before entering he and his horse had been the only living things in the black street.

But I would not run away. It would be a pretty thing to go home to my grandmother and tell her that I was afraid of the house because I could not make Bridget Kelly hear me and had run away in the full sunshine of a June day.

Probably Bridget was upstairs in some one of the forty-six rooms.

From the hall itself four doors of very fine wine-red mahogany opened. I looked into one after the other. They were reception-rooms of great size, so far as I could judge; but the sun was the other side of the house, and only an eastern light came in through the chinks of the window shutters. The rooms were full of sheeted shapes in the dimness. I don't think I could have brought myself to go into them. I know I closed each door with a hasty bang, as though it had been a Blue Beard's Chamber.

As I went upstairs my heels made a great noise on the marble steps. At the head of the stairs I came upon a door which had once been of red baize, although now the baize was in tatters. Beyond it was a long corridor, shuttered like the rest of the house.

I left the baize door open behind me while I peeped fearfully into one room after another whose doors led off from the corridor. These were bedrooms, and it was worse than downstairs. I could see the great four-posters glimmering in the darkness. The smell of mildew was everywhere.

Suddenly my courage gave out. I had an idea. Supposing that Bridget Kelly was lying dead in one of these rooms or the great stone kitchens below!

I turned about hastily, dreading what lay behind me. I would come another time with my godmother. How could one tell who was skulking in the house? The door had been open when I came to it.

And then—I heard the hall door shut with a great bang. There was no wind to shut it. It was the last straw. I fled precipitately through the baize door and on to the staircase, which was lit by a skylight overhead. Even though I met the person who had shut the door I must make towards the sunlight and the world outside.

CHAPTER XVI

THE PORTRAIT

As I came out on to the great landing which had a recess supported by pillars, I saw that a baize door on the other side, corresponding to the one by which I had come was slowly opening. To my excited fancy it opened stealthily, and I stood staring at it, not knowing what might issue from it.

Imagine, then, my joy and surprise when I saw for the second time Anthony Cardew's face. At first I could hardly believe it; and he, on his part, looked equally amazed, and very pleasurably so, I must say.

"Why, where have you dropped from, Miss Bawn?" he asked. "A minute ago I could have sworn I was alone in the house, unless, perhaps, the good old creature who looks after it had come back from her marketing."

"And where have you dropped from?" I asked, suddenly light-hearted. "I thought you were on your way to the South Seas."

"Why so I should have been," he answered, "only for sudden happenings. And how do you come here? To be sure, it is your own house, and I am a trespasser. I little thought when I came who I should find."

"I am in town for a short visit," I said, "with Miss Champion. She was not well to-day so I came to see the house alone."

"And, as luck would have it, I had a fancy on the same day to see a portrait in the picture-gallery here. It is something better than chance, Miss Bawn."

We stood looking at each other with a happy intimacy. And then his mention of the portrait recalled the miniature I had found in the wood. I had had a foolish girl's fancy to hang it about my neck under my dress, and it lay there now, suspended by a slender gold chain which was one of my godmother's gifts to me. I had a shy reluctance to let him know I carried it there.

"By the way," I said, "I believe I have a jewel of yours. I found it in the wood."

His eyes lightened and darkened in a way that was peculiar to him and his cheek flushed.

"You have found the miniature?" he said, in great excitement. "I was heartbroken for the loss of it. Have you got it with you?"

He had stretched out his hand as though he expected his recovered treasure to be handed to him at once, and I could not deny that I had it, so I took it from about my neck, murmuring something about having carried it for safety and that the case was at Aghadoe and should be returned to him.

"I thought you were gone to the ends of the earth," I said lamely; "and I was so afraid that I might lose it before I should have a chance of returning it."

He took it gently and looked at it for a second. Then he kissed it.

"Why, it is warm from its resting-place," he said, "and so the dearer."

And then he took it off from its little chain and placed it in an inner pocket of his coat, handing me back the chain.

"Maybe you'd like to see what picture it was that made me a trespasser," he said, with a suddenly reckless air. "Come, child, and you shall see. Perhaps it was the discovery that the dead was come alive that sent off two decent fellows to find a Spanish galleon without me. There are better things than gold. Aye, faith, the gold on a woman's head, the light in her eye, may be worth many treasure-ships."

We went back through the baize door through which he had come. There was a second door within it which being opened disclosed the picture-gallery; that, being lighted from overhead, had not the gloom of the rest of the house.

I looked around me at the ruffled and periwigged gentlemen, the smiling ladies, who were my ancestors and ancestresses, with interest.

"There is a picture of my grandmother here which I am said to resemble," I said, as I looked down the line of pictures, "though I am ashamed to say that I am thought to resemble her, seeing that she is a great beauty, and is, indeed, beautiful in her old age. Perhaps I resemble her without possessing any of her beauty."

"Ah, Miss Bawn," he said, looking at me roguishly, "'handsome is as handsome does.'"

"That is so," I said. "My grandmother has often told me that if I am good and gentle no one will trouble about my looks."

He turned suddenly then and he said in a singularly sweet voice—

"Dear child! dear child!"

Then he took my hand as though I had been indeed a child and led me up to the portrait.

"What do you see?" he asked.

"I never could be like anything so beautiful," I said, with indignation. "If Gran looked like that she must have been beautiful indeed, and she must have looked like it."

The young girl in the portrait was wearing a white satin gown. She was painted in the manner of the period, with a lamb beside her which she had wreathed with roses; and she stood in a flowery meadow. She had an armful of roses like Flora's self, and as she stood one or two escaped and fell down her dress. She had the long neck which has come to me, a beautiful small head, golden hair, warm fair colouring and violet eyes.

"I never could be like it," I said again.

Captain Cardew smiled. I saw him take the miniature from his pocket and look at it and again at the portrait as though he compared them.

"You see the likeness, do you not?" he asked.

"Yes, there is a likeness," I acknowledged.

"I came here to feast my eyes upon it," he said. "I was frantic at the loss of the miniature. I had seen this picture before, long ago, when I was a boy. When I first saw ... the original of the miniature I remembered this and thought it the strangest coincidence. I wanted to find out for myself if the likeness was really so strong."

"And it was?" I asked.

"It was. Yet you are more like the miniature than the portrait is."

"Ah, no," I said. "I could not be. The portrait is very beautiful."

"You are more like her," he repeated.

We had left the doors of the gallery ajar, and now we heard plainly a heavy foot coming up the stairs and puffing and wheezing as of a very stout, asthmatic person ascending.

"It is Bridget Kelly," he said, turning and smiling at me. "She was much disturbed that I would not have her as cicerone, but she remembered me from the old days, and, seeing that I would not have her, she left me to mind the house while she did her marketing."

"I found the door open when I came to it," I said.

"Bridget must have left it so. I dare say the house has a ghostly reputation and is shunned. And now, do you know why I did not go treasure-hunting?"

"How should I know?" I answered him.

He caught me suddenly into his arms.

"Because, Bawn, my darling," he said, "the dead has come alive again."

CHAPTER XVII

THE WILL OF OTHERS

He let me go gently just as the old foot touched the top step of the stairs, and Bridget Kelly, a little, fat, rosy, smiling woman, much pleasanter of expression than her sister, Maureen, came into the gallery.

"Why, bless me, Captain Cardew," she said, "who have you found? There is a cabman at the door who would have it that he was waiting for a young lady, although I told him no young lady had come in but only a gentleman."

"Look and see who it is, Bridget," Captain Cardew answered her.

She looked at me in a momentary bewilderment. Then she flung her arms about me.

"Why, it must be Miss Bawn," she cried. "Miss Bawn, and the image of her Ladyship, yet more red in the cheeks than her Ladyship had, except maybe when his Lordship was courting her. And where did you come from at all, Miss Bawn? or did the sky open to let you fall through?"

"I came by the cab, Bridget. I am in Dublin on a visit with Miss Champion. You remember Miss Champion?"

"Is it Miss Mary? Aye, troth, I do remember her. 'Tis mistress of this house she ought to be by rights, leastways when his Lordship and her Ladyship are gone to their rest; and long may it be before they go! So you're here with Miss Mary, Miss Bawn, honey? And wasn't it the quarest thing at all that you should walk into the house and find Captain Anthony in it?"

"I was nearly running out of it," I said. "I was frightened of all the empty rooms. The sound of the hall door shutting frightened me most of all. I was about to run out of the house when I met Captain Cardew."

"Ah, sure, and you weren't frightened then?" the old woman said in a coaxing way. "You wouldn't be frightened with Captain Anthony to take care of you? No lady would. Sure, dear, I've lived in it many a year my lone self, and worse than myself I've never seen, though they do have quare ould stories about it. I wouldn't be frightened, itself, if I did see anything, only spake bouldly to it and ax it what was keepin' it from its rest."

"My grandmother will be glad to hear you are well, Bridget. She told me to be sure to see you. She sent you some presents. You will find a parcel in the cab at the door."

"Her Ladyship is always kind and good, the Lord reward her! I think I'll be gettin' down to see her and the Abbey and Maureen before the winter comes. And now, Miss Bawn, you'll be seein' the house?"

I felt that it would be the greatest unkindness to refuse her, so we made the journey of all the forty-two rooms, and in every one Bridget had stories to tell, and she pointed to the pictures and the bric-a-brac and the tapestries, and classified the furniture, like any guide-book.

I was not as excited about them as otherwise I might have been. Indeed, I could think of nothing but that Anthony Cardew was beside me, and that he had clasped me in his arms and kissed me and that there was no gentleman on earth his equal.

I knew now how foolish it was about Theobald, and how impossible it was that our brotherly and sisterly intimacy could ever have ripened into love. Indeed, I felt years older than Theobald, and I said to myself that never in any circumstances could I have cared for a boy like him. As we went from room to room my heart felt as though it were on wings. To see Captain Cardew, how polite and kind he was to old Bridget, opening and closing the shutters for her and helping her up and down steps, filled me with pride and joy. Was it possible that he could care for a little ignorant girl like me, this preux chevalier, who had been secretly a hero of romance to me as long as I remembered?

All the time as we went Bridget talked incessantly, although she became scanter and scanter of breath. She had all sorts of reminiscences of my grandfather and grandmother and of the great days in the house; but I noticed that once when she mentioned Uncle Luke's name she coughed to cover her mistake, and looked oddly from Captain Cardew to me as though she wondered at finding us together.

And then we were taken down to the drawing-room which opened on the right-hand side of the hall; and she would take off the covers of the old French furniture to show us the beautiful old chintzes with which they were upholstered. Also she would have us admire the Italian mantelpieces inlaid with coloured marble, and the decoration of the walls and ceilings which were very fine indeed, and the picture by Angelica Kauffmann of the Lady St. Leger of that day as St. Cecilia playing on her organ, and the other beautiful things which the rooms contained. All the time she sighed over the years during which the house had been closed up.

"Sure, it's time it was all forgotten," she said, "and that his Lordship and her Ladyship came back to where many a one would welcome them. It was fine, Miss Bawn, when the wax lights were lit in all the chandeliers and the flashing of them was nearly as fine as the ladies' diamonds. There used to be the height of fashion and beauty here but never one that I'd compare to her Ladyship. Ah, sure, they were great days!"

"And who knows but they may come again?" said Anthony Cardew.

We were in the inner drawing-room by this time, and as it happened there was a picture of Theobald as a little boy sitting on his pony, above the fireplace.

A memory came back to me, out of the mists of childhood, of Theobald sitting astride the little shaggy pony. I had quite forgotten it, but now I remembered even the pony's name, which was Orson. And there was a distracted person in a velvet coat, who must have been the artist; and he implored Theobald to keep still, for he would touch up Orson and set him prancing. It was on the lawn near the yew-hedge, and I was standing by my grandmother, while Theobald on the pony was on the gravel-sweep. I knew that he made the pony curvet because I liked it; and presently my grandmother discovered that and took me away.

"Sure, the fine days will come back," the old woman assented hopefully, "and there's the bonny boy'll bring them. Miss Bawn, dear, when is Master Theobald coming home from the wars to marry you? Weren't you promised from the cradle? Sure, old as I am, I'll dance at the wedding."

To my vexation I felt the colour rush to my face and I was conscious that Captain Cardew was looking at me in a startled way.

I tried to say something to the effect that it was an arrangement which we should probably never desire to carry out, but, forcing myself to look at Captain Cardew, I was silenced by the cold and stern expression of his face.

I saw him go up and examine the portrait, and then turn away. I looked at him piteously. In spite of old Bridget's presence I had almost courage to put my hand in his and say to him that he was the only man on earth for me.

But he was holding the door open now for Bridget and me to pass through and he would not meet my eyes. And the old woman was begging me to be seated awhile till she made me a cup of tea and was inviting him similarly. He refused, saying he had business elsewhere. And then he took my hand and lifted it coldly to his lips; and shaking old Bridget by the hand he was gone.

As the door slammed behind him, again the cold chill of the house struck me for the sunshine had gone with him. I realized my own unreadiness too late, and I could have followed him, calling out to him till he should turn round and come back and hear me tell him that it was all foolishness about Theobald and I loved only him. Indeed, I got so far as to run out to the postern gate and look down the street.

But it was as lifeless as when I had come in. There was only my cab, and the driver dozing on the box and the patient horse standing quietly between the shafts to break the dead monotony of the lines of black houses.

CHAPTER XVIII.

FLIGHT

I drank Bridget's strong, sweet tea without protest, and ate the thin bread and butter, feeling it taste like sawdust in my mouth.

Meanwhile, the good old soul sat and looked at me with a beaming expression.

"I little thought," she said, "when I rose up this morning, honey-jewel, of who'd be here before the day was over. Sure, you're pale, love! Maybe 'twas tiring you I was, trapesin' through the house. Maureen 'ud have something to say to me. She was always terrible jealous of her babies."

I assured her I was not tired. I tried to talk to her about Maureen and the Abbey and my grandparents, and all the time I felt that she watched me with an anxious and fond gaze.

"I wouldn't be telling her Ladyship, if I was you, Miss Bawn," she said suddenly, "about meeting Captain Anthony Cardew here. 'Twould vex her, so it would. I was surprised to find you talking together. 'Twas the unluckiest thing in the world that you and him should meet."

"I had met Captain Cardew before, Bridget," I said coldly. "He had rendered me a service. I'm sure all that old trouble ought to be forgotten, and I think my grandmother is too good a Christian, and too reasonable to bear Captain Cardew enmity for something which was no fault of his."

"That may be, dearie," old Bridget said, with the fond, coaxing way of our people towards us. "That may be. Still, if I was you, Miss Bawn, I wouldn't think of Captain Anthony, even if he did do you a service. He's a beautiful gentleman, and many a lady was mad for him, I know well, and not his fault either; and many a poor girl, too, because he was so pleasant. And no woman had ever cause to blame him or do anything but love him. Still, dear, Master Theobald's the husband for you. Isn't he young and bonny, like yourself? And Captain Cardew has a white head. He's old by you, Miss Bawn."

I remembered the old, childish days when she had been tenderer to me than Maureen, and she looked at me so wistfully that I could not be angry with her. Indeed, I could have almost wept, like the child of long ago, on her comfortable breast. And I was hardly vexed that she called Anthony Cardew old. What did it matter, since I loved him, and he would always, always be the finest gentleman in the world to me?

I kissed her and left her, promising to come again and to bring Miss Champion with me, and I drove back in the cab to St. Stephen's Green. At one moment my heart was heavy because Captain Cardew was angry with me; and at another it was irrationally light, because he loved me and breathed the same air with me. Was it only a few hours ago since we had been almost strangers and I had believed him far away at the ends of the earth? And how the world had changed for him and for me since! To be sure, I had been unready, and I realized now that I had no address which should find him. But I could find out where he was. Why, any second I might meet him in these streets! And the mere possibility made them blossom like the rose. Men like Anthony Cardew did not easily hide themselves. I would find him, and the foolish misunderstanding would be cleared up. As for the other difficulties, what did they matter since we loved each other? I had that happy confidence in him that he would sweep through obstacles as a bright sword through a maze of thorns.

When I arrived at St. Stephen's Green, expecting to find my godmother sleeping or at least resting, I found her, to my amazement, up and bustling about, and her maid packing our trunks.

"Why, how long you have been, Bawn!" she said; "and I wanted you, child. We are going home this evening. There will be just time to catch the six o'clock express. Louise has packed for you, and we can dine in the train."

"But why, why?" I asked, cold dismay seizing on my heart.

"I will tell you presently. Poor Bawn, what a shame that your gaieties should be interrupted! I would leave you behind me, if I could. But perhaps we shall return."

She drew me to her and kissed me. Of course she could say no more, since Louise was in the room; but glancing at the dressing-table, which was now stripped of its pretty things in silver and tortoise-shell, a letter addressed in my grandmother's handwriting caught my eye. It must have come since I went out; and there must be something in it to explain our sudden departure.

"There is nothing wrong at Aghadoe, is there?" I asked, in sharp fear.

"I should have told you, Bawn, if there was. They are quite well."

I went out of the room into my own little room, where my trunks stood in the middle, locked and labelled. The letter must have come immediately after I had gone out. What could it contain that necessitated this hurried flight? I looked around the little room where I had been happy for a fortnight, and my eyes filled with tears. I had a feeling that I should not come back to it.

While I stood there, miserably, I heard a knock at the hall door, without attaching any significance to it. There was nothing left for me to do—everything had been done for me; so I sat down in my hat and jacket as I was, and gave myself up to a bitter regret. At the moment it seemed the hardest and cruellest thing in the world that I should be taken away from the place which held Anthony Cardew—where I might meet him at any moment—and, so far as I could see, since my grandparents were well, without adequate cause.

I had a sudden feeling as though they, as though my godmother, must know that I loved Anthony Cardew and that he loved me in return. Of course, it was impossible; but it seemed to be a foretaste of the opposition I should have to face; and, although I could face it for his sake, yet it struck me coldly that I should ever be in opposition to the will of those who loved me so tenderly.

There was a tap at the door, and the little maid of the house came in, with a sad face, to say that the cab was come.

"And, Miss Bawn," she added, "I found this in the letter-box for you, when I went to call the cab."

I took the letter from her hand and my heart gave a great leap. I had never seen my beloved's handwriting, but I had not a doubt that it was his. Ah, so he had not left me in suspense! He had written to me to tell me, surely, that he understood. He was not one to let a misunderstanding come between us. How fortunate it was that I had told him where we were! He must have left the letter himself. He had been so near me, and I had not known.

I put down the letter with an indifferent air till the little maid had left the room. When she had gone I snatched it up and was about to read it, when my godmother called me, and then I thrust it into my bosom unread. I placed it over my heart and it felt warm there. It brought me into touch with him, so that, after all, it was not so bitter to be going since I could write. And the very keeping back the reading of the letter was sweet.

I was able to face my godmother with a smiling face, although I've no doubt my eyes still bore the traces of tears.

"You are a dear child, Bawn," she said, lifting my face by the chin, and looking down into my eyes, "a dear child!"

I felt a hypocrite at her praises, for I had been in flat rebellion a little while before, and it was only the letter that had enabled me to lift up my heart; but her mind was too occupied for her to notice how my eyes fell and the guilty expression I must have worn.

A minute later we were in the cab, and I was watching the stream of people in the street eagerly to see if I might see Anthony Cardew's face among them. But I did not see any one at all resembling him.

And presently we were in the train and had a carriage to our two selves; and when the train had started my godmother took out of her handbag my grandmother's letter.

"I am going to let you read this, Bawn," she said, "for I think you are of an age now to be taken into our difficulties. I confess it puzzles me."

CHAPTER XIX

THE CRYING IN THE NIGHT

"My dearest daughter," the letter began; it was so my grandmother always addressed Mary Champion. "We are pleased with the fine accounts of how Bawn is enjoying herself and your gaieties and the old friends you have met. The house is very lonely without Bawn, and I miss your coming, and there has been no letter from Theobald since you went. Perhaps Bawn has had one. We seem to realize that we are old and our children dead and their children away from us, all at once."

The letter went on to talk of trivial and ordinary things, but my grandmother was bad at deception, and one felt that her thoughts were not in the things she told, but that they were written with an intention to conceal something. And at last the thin deception gave way.

"Mr. Dawson has been to see Lord St. Leger," ran the last paragraph. "He had some astounding news. And Mrs. Dawson has driven over to call, and we are to dine with them next week. I wish you were home, Mary. I want you to lean upon."

When I had read I turned amazed eyes on my godmother.

"The Dawsons!" I said. "And we used always to say that though every other house in the county were opened to the Dawsons, Aghadoe Abbey would shut its door in their faces."

"It shall shut its door," Mary Champion said indignantly. "He is frightening them because they are old and have no son to lean upon. Garret Dawson is an evil plotter and schemer, and there is blood and tears on his money. Aghadoe shall be safe from him."

"How can he have frightened them?" I asked. "They have never borrowed money from him."

The cloud deepened on my godmother's face.

"It must be something about Luke," she said. "But whatever it is, I will swear it is not true. Luke never did anything that would put his old father and mother in the power of Garret Dawson. He has frightened them because I was not there to protect them. I shall tear through his web of lies."

As she said it the light came to her eyes and the colour to her lips, and I wondered that any one could ever have thought her plain.

"So you see, Bawn," she said, as she took the letter from me and folded it up, "there was cause for our return. You know I would not take you away from your enjoyment without cause."

"Yes, I knew that," I said.

Indeed, when we reached Aghadoe my grandmother was so tremulous in her joy at seeing us, and she clung so to Mary Champion, that we might have been away two years instead of two weeks.

It was late when we arrived, and there was supper prepared for us; and while we ate it my grandfather sat in his chair by the window, where we could not see his face, and was silent. There was a gloom over the meal, a sense of trouble impending. It was not at all a joyful occasion as it ought to have been, since we had come back. My grandmother hovered about us uneasily, pressing this and that thing upon us, for she had bidden Neil Doherty to lock up and go to bed, saying that we could wait on ourselves, to his manifest indignation. And presently my grandfather got up, excused himself for being tired, and, having kissed my godmother and me on our cheeks, went away with a tired and uncertain step.

Something had happened. It was obvious that there was a sense of it in the faces of the old servants. Even Dido whimpered uneasily under my caressing hand.

My grandmother remembered to ask me if I had heard from Theobald, and it was only then, with a sense of shame, that I realized the absence of Theobald's letters and the fact that I had not noticed their absence. Why, I had not written to Theobald for several weeks past; but I did not dare to tell my grandmother so. Of course there were many reasons why Theobald should not have written. He was very gay in India, much in demand in his spare time for all sorts of entertainments.

"If there had been any serious reason for his not writing we should have heard fast enough, Gran," I said.

"Why, that is true, Bawn," she replied. "Still, where one loves one is unnecessarily anxious."

I felt the rebuke of her words, though I knew she had intended no rebuke, and made up my mind with a rush of compunction to write a long letter to Theobald in the morning.

Miss Champion was staying the night at Aghadoe; and I thought it would be well to leave her and my grandmother together that they might talk over things. Besides that, I had not yet read my letter and the moment was approaching when I might do so. And all at once my patience seemed to have given out, to be quite exhausted. So I took my bedroom candle and went.

When I had reached my own room I locked the door lest by any chance I should be disturbed; although that did not seem likely. I lit four candles and made quite an illumination in the great, dim room. Then I took the letter from where it had lain all day over my heart, and I set it on the table in the candle-light. I got into a loose gown and slippers with a kind of painful, yet sweet deliberation. Now that the moment had come for my joy I dallied with it.

My first love-letter! I realized all at once that Theobald's fond, boyish epistles had no real, man's love in them. I was only the dear companion, the sister, to him. I was sure of it, else I had been very unhappy.

Then I took the letter and held it to the candle-light with a throbbing heart. And this is what I read:

"My dear Miss Bawn,

"For a moment I forgot my white head and my years, and for that foolish presumption you must pardon me and never think less kindly of me. From your old servant's lips I learned the truth: that you had a lover of your own age, whom I pray God may be worthy of you. After all, since my dream of treasure here was but a dream, I have reconsidered my refusal, and shall join the expedition in search of mere earthly treasure. If we never meet again, think kindly of him who would die for you.

"Your faithful friend and servant,
"Anthony Cardew."

I was like one who has had a blow and a bad one, and I felt a curious quietness steal upon me and numb me. Despite the sweet, warm air of the summer night I was cold. In the quietness I heard the Abbey clock strike twelve; I heard soft stirrings in the leaves outside; a thousand little sounds which I would not have noticed at another time, that were distinct in the stillness that had come upon me.

I went on making my preparations for bed as though nothing had happened. I omitted nothing, but all the time I felt as though I were somehow outside my body and knew the dull numbness of it as a thing apart.

When I was ready at last I unlocked the door so that the maid who came with my morning tea and my bath-water should not find it locked. Then I blew out the candles, and, taking the letter in my hand, I crept into bed.

That night I was awakened by the crying in the shrubbery outside which I had not heard for a long time, and I listened to it, cold in the darkness, till the cocks began crowing and then it ceased. I knew that the ghosts always came for trouble at Aghadoe, and I prayed hard that the trouble might be only mine and might spare the two dear old people. The thought of Theobald, and that I had not even noticed the absence of his letters, stung me sharply. What if harm should come to Theobald? As the cocks crew and the grey turned to blue and then to gold in the room, I lay staring up at the ceiling, praying that harm had not come to Theobald, that he might be well and happy although I must be miserable for ever.

CHAPTER XX

AN EAVESDROPPER

The morning sun was in my room when I awoke and my godmother was by my bed.

"You have been crying in your sleep, Bawn," she said. "I thought I heard you several times during the night, but was not sure. Are you anxious about Theobald, child?"

"There is some trouble in the air," I said, turning away my head. "But I don't think it was I who cried."

"I would not say that to Lady St. Leger, Bawn," she said, lifting my face and making me look at her.

"It is not for a death," I said, "or we should have heard the coach."

"God forbid!" I noticed that her face had a new look of care since yesterday, that there were rings round her fine eyes as though she had not slept. "Yet it may be bad enough, although not for a death."

"What is it?"

"Why, Bawn, child, that is the strangest thing of all. You are no longer a child, Bawn, and I bring my burden to you to lighten it by sharing. They will not tell me what the trouble is."

"Not tell you!"

I was amazed. For so long I had known Mary Champion as the stay and support of my grandparents that I could hardly believe there was anything they would keep from her.

"They will not tell me," she repeated. "Your grandmother says that it is Lord St. Leger's will that I am not to be told. It is something they must endure together. I know it is something about Luke. If they will not tell me I shall go and ask Garret Dawson why he is frightening them and with what."

"Grandpapa would never forgive you," I said.

The shadow fell deeper on her face.

"I know he would not," she said. "Must I wait for them to speak, then, lest I should do harm?"

"I think you must wait for them to speak."

"If it was a mere matter of money"—she wrung her hands together in a way which in a person of her calm, benignant temperament suggested great distress—"if it were a mere matter of money, I would sell Castle Clody—yes, every stick and stone of it. But I think it is more than money. I shall ask Lord St. Leger to tell me. It is not fair that I, who ought to have been Luke's wife and their daughter, should be kept in the dark."

She went away and left me then, and I got up and dressed with a heavy heart, which all the chorus of the birds and the sweet green of the trees and grass and the delicious scents and sounds outside could not charm from its heaviness.

At breakfast, although my godmother did her best, talking about old friends we had met in Dublin and delivering their messages to Lord and Lady St. Leger, and although I tried to do my part, the gloom was as marked as the gloom last night. My grandfather and grandmother sat side by side at the round table, and now and again they looked at each other like people who were absorbed in grave anxieties to the exclusion of what went on about them.

I thought that my grandfather had, all of a sudden, begun to show his age. He was not so far from eighty, but hitherto he had been hale and active, so that one would have credited him with many years less. But now he seemed shaky and tremulous, as my grandmother had been last night. His blue eyes had a film of trouble over them, as I remembered to have seen them when I was a child and there was the trouble about Uncle Luke. I had noticed it then with a childish wonder, although I had forgotten about it till now.

After breakfast he went out to the garden with my grandmother and walked up and down with her on the terrace in the sun.

"I am going to see if they will not tell me, Bawn," my godmother said presently, standing up. "And I shall not rest till I have found out. Garret Dawson will find it a very different thing to frighten me. Your grandfather is very old, Bawn, or this would not have happened."

She went after them, and I saw her take an arm of each and go down the garden with them, they leaning on her.

When they were out of sight I went into the library to write my letter to Theobald, taking the blotting-pad and pen and ink and paper to my favourite seat in the oriel. There presently my godmother found me. I was getting on but slowly with the letter, for my unhappy thoughts were grinding upon each other like the stones of a quern, trying to find a solution of something that could not be solved.

"Lord St. Leger would do everything but tell me the whole truth," she said. "Poor souls! They think I ought not to be told evil of Luke, as though I were not the one to say that I did not believe it. There is something of money in it, but there is worse than money. What is one to do in this darkness? They don't see how cruel it is to me, to keep me in the dark. I have to be patient with them because they are so old."

Then she stooped and kissed me.

"I must go back to Castle Clody now," she said. "I wonder how my baby has done without me? She does worse without me than she thinks."

I had heard her before call her cousin her baby, and indeed it was true that Miss Joan depended on her for everything.

Then her eye fell on my letter, and she asked me if I were writing to Theobald; and when I answered her that I was she put her hand on my head and told me not to be anxious about Theobald, because she was sure he was all right and that a letter was only delayed.

"Don't lose your beauty-sleep any more, Bawn," she said, "for I am sure there is a letter on its way. All this has spoilt your looks since yesterday."

As the day went on it grew very hot. All the windows were open, without making the room cooler; there was a sleepy sound of insects in the grass outside. Bees droned in and out of the window. White clouds sailed across the sky; and a soft, warm wind rustled the leaves with a sound like rain upon them.

I remember closing my eyes and leaning my head against the window-shutter. I suppose I was tired after the wakefulness of the night. Anyhow, I must have fallen asleep and slept a couple of hours.

When I began to wake the sky had become gloomy and overcast, but it was as hot as ever, and there was someone talking close at hand, a low, quiet talking which at first mixed with my dreams and was a part of them.

Presently I recognized the fact that I must have fallen asleep over the letter to Theobald, and also that the voice, the voices, near me were those of my grandfather and grandmother.

I had no intention to eavesdrop, but I was drowsy and for a moment or two I nodded again.

"But why should Luke have borrowed money from Jasper Tuite?" my grandmother said. "He could have had what he liked from us."

"He had as handsome an allowance as I could afford to give him," my grandfather said, "and he knew that he could have come to me in a difficulty."

"And why should Garret Dawson spring it on us at this time of day?" my grandmother went on. "Why should he frighten us with it now that we are old, and have no son to lean upon?"

"Because he wants the money, and I wonder he has gone without it so long. And also because we have not opened our doors to him nor accepted his invitations. He is determined that we shall assist at his triumph."

"And we must do it?"

"We must do it, else he will publish the boy's disgrace."

"And must Bawn go with us, Toby?"

"Yes; we have to do it thoroughly. The invitation included Bawn. She will not feel it as we shall; and she knows nothing of our cause for unhappiness."

"She does not look over-happy," my grandmother said, and sighed. "I wish Theobald were home and that they were married."

"Poor Theobald! poor boy! We have placed him in Garret Dawson's power. When you and I are gone, Theobald and Bawn will be homeless, unless we can propitiate this man to spare them; and I have heard it said that Garret Dawson has as much mercy in his heart as a tiger. But I had to sign, dear; you know I had to sign."

"My poor Toby, I know!"

A silence followed; I did not dare to stir, to betray my presence. But presently they got up and went away, and when I heard the slow steps die away in the distance I went out by the open window to ponder over what I had heard.

CHAPTER XXI

THE NEW MAID

I went away to that glade in the wood of happy memories to think things out, and dropped down there amid the flowers of which it was full, with my eyes fixed on the wood-anemones and violets without seeing them.

Troubles were coming, indeed, so thick and fast that my mind was in a confusion. I did not know whether to tell my godmother or not what I had overheard. She had a straight way of going to the root of things. Supposing that she did as she had threatened, and went to Dawson himself for the truth, might she not exasperate him into making public the thing which had so much power to frighten Lord and Lady St. Leger? I had gathered that there was disgrace hanging over us, disgrace, and homelessness for Theobald and me. Aghadoe Abbey was dear to us as flesh and blood. Was it possible that it could pass away from us into the possession of the Dawsons? Why, I would a thousand times rather that fire had it and that it should be consumed to ashes.

It should have been a small thing by comparison that my grandfather had said I was to go to the Dawsons' dinner-party, but I had so violent an aversion to going that the matter really bulked large in the list of troubles. I should not mind so much if Richard Dawson were not present, and of course it might be that already he had found us too dull and had gone away on his wanderings.

But this little hope of mine was destined very soon to be extinguished.

I have not said that old Dido was with me, but, since she was my constant companion this was to be expected. She had followed me to the glade, and was lying with her head on the end of my skirt, at peace, since she was with me. Away from me or my grandmother or Miss Champion she would whimper and shiver like a lonely old ghost in a world of living things.

Suddenly as I sat there, thinking, she crept close to me with a low growl. I had not heard a sound except the songs of the birds and the stir of the south wind in the leaves that was like the placid flowing of waters. I put my hand on her head and she bristled under my hand, but she was quiet. She would always be quiet with my hand upon her head.

I wondered if it were a wild cat or a weazel or a stoat that had so excited her. But I was not long in suspense. There came a murmur of voices and a man's laugh. Then there were footsteps. I had a vague alarm. Who could it be that walked in our woods and set Dido bristling? She was a gentle creature and knew her friends; and the people about were all kind and friendly to "Master Luke's" old dog.

I threw a fold of my skirt over her head to keep her from hearing, and, with my hand on her collar, I moved as close as I could to the leafy screen that separated the glade from the wood-path.

There was a couple coming up the path; presently they were in my view, and I saw to my grief and amazement that the man was Richard Dawson—I had known it, indeed, from the first—and the girl who walked with him was Nora Brady, the pretty little girl who had interested me at Araglin Creamery. Richard Dawson walked with his arm about her. She was looking up at him as though she adored him. Just as they passed he bent his head and kissed her and again I heard him laugh. The laugh made me hate him, if possible, more than ever.

I guessed that they had come in by the postern gate and would return that way, and I did not dare to stir till they had come back again. They did not, however, take so long. They came back again very soon, whispering as they had gone; and as soon as I judged it safe I left the glade and hurried home as fast as ever I could resolving to have the postern gate bolted so that Richard Dawson should not dare to come into our woods, and resolving also to see and speak with Nora Brady as soon as ever I had a chance. Perhaps, indeed, she would not listen to me, but I could only do my best.

As it happened, my opportunity came sooner than I had expected; for it was only next day that I met her coming with a basket of eggs to the Abbey.

She dropped me a curtsey and would have passed on, but I stopped her. We were all alone in the wide avenue, as much alone to all intents and purposes as we could have been anywhere. I went straight to the point, feeling the painfulness of having to speak and doing it as directly as possible.

"Nora," I said, "I am only a girl like yourself, so don't be frightened of me. I always thought you a good girl, Nora, but I saw you walking yesterday in the wood with Mr. Dawson of Damerstown, and you were like lovers, and that ought not to be so unless you are going to marry him."

"Oh, Miss Bawn!"

Poor Nora's face was covered with confusion, and I am sure I blushed as hotly as she did, yet I was conscious of a cold, shrinking feeling from this courtship between her and Richard Dawson which I was sure could lead to no good.

"It isn't right, Nora," I said.

"God help me! I know that, Miss Bawn," she said, looking at me with frightened eyes. "I've tried to give it up; I've tried to resist him, but I can't. There's something stronger than myself that drives me to him. I love him, Miss Bawn, so I do; and I can't help it that he's a rich gentleman and I'm only a poor girl. If you ever loved any one yourself, Miss Bawn, you'd know."

"I do know, Nora," I said. I knew that if Anthony Cardew lifted his finger to me I would follow him over the world. "I do know. But it can only end in misery, unless Mr. Dawson were willing to marry you."

"He has never said a word about marriage. But you mustn't think he's bad, Miss Bawn. 'Tis my own fault, for I love him so much, and he can't help seeing it. But he's never said a word he mightn't say to a lady. There's the kissing—"

"Yes, there's the kissing. It oughtn't to be, Nora." As I said it I felt what a poor hypocrite I was, for I could never have resisted Anthony Cardew if he had wished to kiss me, never, never, no matter what trouble or misery it involved. "You ought to go away, Nora, out of the reach of temptation. There is no one dependent on you; no one for whose sake you need dread to go. The only thing would be to go away."

"I've thought of it, Miss Bawn, but sure, if he wanted me I'd only have to come back."

There was something in her voice that frightened me; it sounded so hopeless, so without any capacity for resistance.

"My aunt is own maid to Lady Garmoy," she went on. "She could get me a place in her ladyship's household, under herself. I might go, but, Miss Bawn, I'd never know the day nor the hour he mightn't draw me back to him. All the same, you mustn't think me a bad girl, Miss Bawn. It isn't right for him or for me; sure, I know it isn't. I can't say my prayers as I used to. But if I went among strangers I couldn't tell the day or the hour it 'ud be too much for me, and I'd be stealing out of the house and taking the train back. It isn't as if there was someone I could tell, some one that would hold me, that I could run to when the fit was on me."

"Nora," I said, with a sudden thought, "how would it be if you were to come to me? My grandmother will let me have a maid of my own when I want one. Come to me, and Bridget Connor will teach you your duties, and you will have the little room off mine to sit and sew in. You need never go outside the Abbey gates if you do not care to. The place is big enough to walk about in. And if you are hard pressed you can run to me, Nora. You will feel that I am just a girl like yourself, and will not be afraid. And I shall hold your hands till the danger is past."

"May the Lord reward you, Miss Bawn!"

"Then I may speak to Lady St. Leger?"

"I shall love to be with you, Miss Bawn. Sure, there isn't anything I wouldn't do for you. He'll never know where I am, no more than if I'd slipped off to my aunt at Lady Garmoy's. I need never be leaving the Abbey unless to go to Mass on a Sunday, and he'll never know anything about that. 'Tis for his sake as much as my own. 'Tisn't right that he should be making love to a poor girl."

I stooped down and kissed Nora on the cheek. It seemed incredible that Richard Dawson should have filled Nora's innocent heart with much the same feeling that I had for Anthony Cardew, but I said nothing. Who is to answer for such things?

"I will come back with you now and speak to Lady St. Leger," I said.

CHAPTER XXII

THE DINNER PARTY

The day following that Nora became an inmate of Aghadoe. She had no relative nearer than an uncle, who had a houseful of children of his own, so that Nora's absence must be a relief in a manner of speaking; and my grandmother never refused me anything in reason. Nora was modest and dainty in her ways, and having been brought up by the nuns she was an excellent needlewoman, so that she had so much equipment for the post of my maid.

The day came round on which we were to dine at Damerstown. I had not meant to tell Nora that we were going there, but she discovered it from something my grandmother said when she came to my room, and I noticed that she sat with tightly compressed lips over her sewing that afternoon.

She had put out my dress for me by my orders. I had chosen the least becoming garment in my wardrobe, a black grenadine, very simply made, which belonged to my schoolgirl days. It was high to the neck and had elbow sleeves, and the cut was old-fashioned. I wished to look my worst at Damerstown, although I was forced to go there by my grandfather's will.

It was nearly time for me to dress when my grandmother came into the little room, where I was sitting watching Nora as she sewed a little tucker of old lace into the neck of the garment.

"What are you going to wear, Bawn?" she asked.

"This." I indicated the grenadine.

"It will never do, Bawn," my grandmother said, shaking her head. "We are to do honour to our hosts. I am wearing my moiré and my diamonds. If you were to appear in this your grandfather would send you back to change."

"I should have thought it good enough for the Dawsons," I said, with a little heat; and then I remembered Nora's presence, and also that my grandparents were frightened of the Dawsons and anxious to propitiate them, and I was sorry.

"What would you like me to wear, Gran?" I asked.

"Your white silk with the Limerick lace."

"Why, I shall be like a bride," I said aghast, for the white silk was one of my godmother's gifts to me, and the finest gown I possessed. When she had given it to me she had said that I should dance in it at a Castle ball.

"Never mind," my grandmother said. "Your grandfather wishes it, child. And you are to wear the pearls. I am going to send Bridget Connor to dress your hair. Nora can do the rest." She turned to smile kindly at Nora. "See you look your best, child. It is your grandfather's will."

Bridget Connor piled my hair in soft, cloudy masses on the top of my head. In and out through the coils she wound a string of my grandmother's pearls. Then she went away, and Nora took her place and helped to dress me.

The white silk had lain by for many a year and was somewhat yellowed, but the richer for that. Louise in adapting it had altered its character but little. It was short in the waist and somewhat narrowly cut, straight and demure all round till it ended in a little train at the back. It was almost swathed in the most beautiful old Limerick lace, through which the rich ivory tints of the silk showed. My grandmother's pearls went three times round my neck before they fell loosely on my bodice.

When I looked at my reflection in the long mirror I confess my splendour rather dazzled me. If only it had been for Anthony Cardew's eyes! But I hated that I should appear so fine to do honour to the Dawsons, and I dreaded more than ever meeting Richard Dawson's insolent gaze.

I wondered how he would take it when he saw me and recognized me for the peasant girl he had insulted. Would he be abashed, confused? I thought he must be; and the one pleasant thing in what was going to befall me was that I should see his discomfiture.

"Miss Bawn, you look as if you'd just come out of heaven," Nora said fervently, as she watched me drawing on my lace mittens.

"I don't feel like it, Nora," I replied, "nor as if I were going there either."

At the last moment something of my grandmother's could not be found, so that we were delayed and arrived at Damerstown on the stroke of eight.

My neighbour at the dinner-table told me afterwards that Mr. Dawson had fidgeted over our late arrival. I thought I could see it in the look of relief with which he came to meet us, and the evident flurry of poor Mrs. Dawson, who was looking fatter than ever in a very tight-fitting, plum-coloured satin, and hotter than ever, despite the incessant waving of her fan.

The long, splendid drawing-room was full of very gaily-dressed ladies, much bejewelled, and many men whose looks did not prepossess me. When I had sat down, under cover of my grandmother, in a chair a little retired behind hers, I looked about me with some dread, and I was glad to recognize the friendly face of Sir Arthur Ardaragh, who came up to us with a cordial greeting. He did not look at all at home among the Dawsons' friends, and I wondered how Lady Ardaragh had persuaded him to come.

For a moment I did not see Lady Ardaragh anywhere, but presently her uplifted voice told me where she was, and looking down I caught a glimpse of her pretty shoulders showing rosily out of a pale green frock. She was talking to someone; I could not see who it was for the moment.

I had not yet seen Richard Dawson; and as my eye went from one to the other of the gentlemen without seeing him, I began to be almost hopeful that he was not there.

Sir Arthur Ardaragh was talking to my grandmother and to Mrs. Dawson, who plainly was too much absorbed by the anxieties of the occasion to hear much of what he was saying. She kept looking with an air of trepidation at her husband who was being effusively polite to my grandfather.

There were only ourselves and the Ardaraghs present of the county-people. The other guests were staying at Damerstown or had come from a distance; they were very fashionable, but I did not like the very low dresses and the loud talk of the ladies, nor the tired, cynical-looking men. Every one of the men, old and young, wore the same expression. I have seen its like since at a foreign Casino, where I watched the baccarat.

The groups broke up as dinner was announced. Mr. Dawson gave his arm to my grandmother. I waited, wondering who might fall to my lot. Then from the group which had been about Lady Ardaragh's chair came—Richard Dawson. He had an air as though he came but half willingly.

Mrs. Dawson, who was going in with my grandfather, turned to me in a great flurry.

"My son will have the honour to take you in, Miss Devereux," she said. The words sounded as though they had been learnt off by heart.

Then Richard Dawson looked at me; and I saw the stupefaction in his eyes. I looked back at him, a direct glance of hatred, as I put my finger-tips gingerly on his sleeve.

"So!" he said in a whisper—"so! What a trick for Fate to play me! And I have been wondering where on earth you had disappeared to. Can you ever forgive me?"

"Never!" I answered, as I went down the marble staircase side by side with him.

CHAPTER XXIII

THE BARGAIN

The memory of that long, dragging, magnificent meal is like a nightmare to me. I loathed it all, the vulgar display of gold plate—I heard afterwards who it was that Garret Dawson had cheated out of it—the number of men-servants, the exotic flowers that made the room sickly, the fruits out of their season.

We are simple people and not accustomed to such banquets; but I was surprised to see how greedy some of the ladies were over the turtle soup, the ortolans and truffles, all the fine things which must have been brought from far off for the dinner. There was an incessant popping of champagne corks, and I wondered at the frequent refilling of the glasses. I did not drink wine, my grandmother did not consider it becoming in a girl, and it seemed the hardest thing in the world to procure a glass of water, judging by the delay in bringing it when I asked for it.

Lady Ardaragh sat nearly opposite to us. I noticed that she was very flushed and her eyes bright, and that she chattered and laughed a great deal.

I had made up my mind that I would not speak to Richard Dawson, although I was forced to sit by him, and that was a contact which I found most detestable. But he would talk to me and sit close to me, and once when I had turned away from him and addressed Sir Arthur Ardaragh, who was on the other side of me, I caught my grandmother's eye on me with a look of appeal.

I wished my godmother had been there. She had been invited to the dinner, but she would not go nor consent to be civil to the Dawsons. Nor would she believe that there was anything about Uncle Luke which might not come into the light of day.

"And if there could be," she said proudly, "I would rather it was told than go in terror of the Dawsons. I had as lief trust the world as them any day."

After that glance of my grandmother I did not turn away again from Richard Dawson, much as I detested his closeness and his breath upon my cheek. I thought the dinner would never be over. As it went on I could not but feel that he was making himself and me conspicuous. He drank a good deal of wine, and the more he drank the more he leant to me and tried to look into my eyes, so that I felt thoroughly sick and ashamed. I could have pushed him away with both hands, but that was not possible in the publicity of a dinner-table. He whispered in my ear, he leant to me, he behaved as an infatuated lover, and presently it seemed to me that my fellow-guests smiled here and there and looked significant. Lady Ardaragh talked more than ever to the blasé-looking young lord who was her neighbour and her colour was heightened. Her witticisms came to me across the table, or a portion of them, and I thought she was saying wild, unbecoming things. I was sure I saw Sir Arthur wince when I turned to him. But it was all too much of a nightmare to myself to be greatly concerned about the feelings of others, even those I liked very much.

At last the welcome signal was given for the ladies to leave the table.

When we had returned to the drawing-room the smart London ladies flocked together in a bevy and began chattering like a field of starlings. Their talk seemed to be altogether of their male acquaintances, whom they called by their names; Jack and Tom and Reggie and Algy, and so on.

Lady Ardaragh sat down by my grandmother and talked to her in a low voice. After the excitement of the dinner she seemed to have become pale and quiet. I could hear that she was talking about her boy, who was a great pet with Gran. I heard her say that he was growing too fast and had been languid of late.

Mrs. Dawson came and sat by me. She sighed with quiet satisfaction as she subsided into her chair.

"It all went off very well, dear," she said, "didn't it? Dawson was very anxious that it should; and I couldn't eat a bit for thinking of what would happen if it didn't go off well."

I answered her that it had gone off very well. It was impossible to dislike her, poor soul; and it was easy to see that she had a wretched life between her husband who was an intolerant tyrant to her and the fine folk he liked to see about him now that his money was made, who were rude and neglectful to her.

"I'm glad you think that, my dear," she said. "Indeed, I think Dawson looked quite cheerful. And I was very glad to see that you and Rick were making friends. He's a very good boy, my dear, although he's a bit wild, having plenty of money and nothing to do but spend it. But he's a very kind boy to his mother. I assure you, dear, there have been times when I wouldn't have cared much to live if it hadn't been for my Rick."

It was a pitiful confession for the mistress of all this splendour; and now that the anxiety and excitement were to some extent over she looked pale and old and tired.

"I'm very glad you liked Rick," she said, "very glad. It isn't like those who would care for him for his money." She nodded her head in the direction of the chattering group. "I should be so glad to see my Rick married to a nice, innocent, good girl. I haven't been so happy this many a day as I've been since I've seen you and him making friends."

I could not bear to tell her that I did not like her son and that nothing on earth would induce me to make friends with him, so I sat silent and said nothing; and I think it did her good to talk, for she prattled on in a gentle, monotonous way about her son's childhood and school-days and of the kindnesses he had done her. Apparently she thought him the finest, handsomest, best person in the world, and apparently his father thought likewise, which was a much stranger thing. She seemed to have no reticence at all, or I had unlocked her heart.

"When Rick is at home," she said, "Dawson is good-tempered, and is often even kind to me. And Rick knows that, and has promised me not to go away any more. I should be so glad if he would marry and settle down, and so would Dawson. There's nothing Dawson wouldn't give him if he'd marry according to his wishes."

At this moment some of the gentlemen arrived, and the group of ladies broke up to admit the black coats. One man passed by and came on towards the end of the room where we were. It was Richard Dawson.

I saw Lady Ardaragh suddenly move her skirt so as to leave a vacant place on the sofa upon which she was sitting; but he disregarded the invitation, if such it were, and came on towards us.

I saw him stoop to kiss his mother and the lighting up of the plain, elderly face, and it came into my mind that however intolerable he was to me, there must be another side of him for her.

For the remainder of that evening he never left my side, and no one could dislodge him, to my great vexation. I thought he was doing it only to annoy me. But I kept close to his mother, so that there was less chance of his making me conspicuous, none at all of his whispering and languishing as he had done at the dinner-table.

I could not see how my grandmother was taking it, since she sat at the same side of the room as I did; but I was glad that Mr. Dawson kept my grandfather in conversation so that he could not see what was going on, for I felt sure that however much he might wish to be civil to the Dawsons, he could not have endured Richard Dawson's attentions to me, since he was very proud.

I have always been one to act on impulse, and of a sudden it occurred to me that it might be possible to make Richard Dawson let poor Nora alone. I suppose it must have been because his mother praised him so much that I should have thought such a thing possible, for up to this I would have believed nothing good of him.

And presently we were alone to all intents, for Mrs. Dawson dropped off to sleep, and the party at the end of the room was playing some noisy round game in which Lady Ardaragh had joined, and Sir Arthur had taken her place beside Gran and they were talking together.

"Mr. Dawson," I said suddenly, "there is something I should like to say to you."

"What is it?"

"Something I should like to ask you."

"Will you come out here on the balcony and ask me what it is? I promise you I shall do it if it be within my power."

The promise determined me. All the windows were wide open, so that to go on the balcony was not to be solitary. As I went out with him I noticed that my grandmother looked after me with an amazed air. Well, I might be mad to believe good of Richard Dawson on his mother's report, but it was worth a trial. I went out on the balcony with him; and noticed that he drew the curtains to after us. It was a thing a gentleman would not have done and I detested him for it. But there was my poor Nora to be thought of, so I endured it.

CHAPTER XXIV

THE BLOW FALLS

"Now, what is it?" he asked. "Half of my fortune if you will, fair lady, so that you forgive that blunder of mine and look kindly on me."

"It is about a girl in whom I am interested—Nora Brady." I felt him start at my side. "I saw you together in our woods the other day. She is a good girl. Mr. Dawson, will you let her be and not make her unhappy?"

"Why," he said, "I have never meant to make her unhappy. I'm sorry for what I did. It was only idle love-making. But she's fond of me, poor child. And she'd be just as fond of me if I wore a ragged coat and earned a shilling a day. I've always pleased myself, and I don't like giving up Nora. By the way, she has rather given up me. She is keeping out of my way. Her keeping out of my way has been more likely to inflame me than the other thing. But, if you'll forgive me and be a little kind to me, I promise you that I won't seek her out."

"What do you want me to do?" I asked.

"More than I dare tell you at present. But for the present, shake hands and say you forgive my rudeness in the wood."

I put my hand in his, and felt his lips upon it, but I bore it.

"Then it is a bargain," he said. "We are enemies no longer, and I promise to let Nora alone. If only the women would always let me alone! What, are you going back to that hot room? And the May moon in the sky, the lovers' moon! Stay with me a little while, because I've been a good boy and promised you what you asked. You could wind me round your little finger. There's nothing I wouldn't do to please you."

The end of his protestations fell on empty air, for I had lifted the curtain and re-entered the drawing-room.

When I came in, with Richard Dawson following me, I was annoyed to find that my grandfather and Mr. Dawson had come into the drawing-room, and were standing near the fireplace. Both looked round, and I thought my grandfather's face wore a startled look, while Mr. Dawson's for an instant beamed excessive gratification.

I hoped that Lord and Lady St. Leger could not think that I tolerated with any patience the attentions of Richard Dawson. Seeing that they believed me bound by some childish promise to my cousin Theobald that was not very likely. And I could not explain to them why I had gone out on the balcony alone with Richard Dawson.

My memory of the time after that seems to consist of nothing but a string of Dawsons coming and going. I did not know what to make of it. Surely the propitiation of the Dawsons did not mean that we should see so very much of them. They were alone now, their fine friends having gone back to London, and their being alone involved an intimacy which need not have been if there were a crowd.

My godmother at this time was much occupied, her cousin, Miss Joan, having developed a disease which in time was to prove mortal, so she knew less of how much the Dawsons came and went, though she must have known it, for I've no doubt the county talked of it. We had been so sure that we would never admit the Dawsons no matter what anyone else did, nor any persons who were merely rich. We had always been very proud and exclusive at Aghadoe.

A little while after that dinner at Damerstown Nora confessed to me with tears that she had stolen out in my absence and had lain in wait for Richard Dawson.

"And after all, Miss Bawn," she said, "I was punished, for he only lifted his hat to me and rode away; and I felt as if I must fall in the track of his horse's feet and implore him to kiss me as he used to. And he never looked back, Miss Bawn."

"I am glad to hear it," I said, feeling that the words were hard and cold.

"I don't know what's come over him," poor Nora said miserably, "unless that, maybe, a good love has come to him at last. I'd just as soon be dead, Miss Bawn."

Soon after that she began talking of going to America, and I used to notice that she looked strangely at me. But I never saw what everyone else must have seen; partly, no doubt, because of that old troth between Theobald and me which I thought my grandparents held to be binding. I ought to have mentioned in its proper place that there had been no cause for Theobald's weeks of silence, or but a trifling one, and that his letters came as of old and were very full of gay doings. I noticed that he did not talk now so much of coming back as he had done at first; but at first he had been very lonely for Aghadoe and all of us.

Day by day during that summer the shadow seemed to darken on Lord St. Leger's face, and my grandmother looked no less harassed. It was, indeed, cruel to see the faces which had been placid enough, despite the lines of sorrow, becoming so haggard and careworn. I used to hate to see them so anxiously polite to Garret Dawson, so willing to sit at his table and have him at theirs. I noticed, too, that they looked strangely at me at times; and I found my grandmother in tears more than once. It hurt me that she should weep at her age.

Another thing I noticed was that they ceased to talk of Theobald; and when his letters came they would read them without comment, or they would take my news of him without an eager stretching forth of their hands for the letter as of old. In those days mysteries seemed to gather thick and fast about me. And I had my own trouble to bear as well. I used to think that Captain Cardew would have made short work of it all. He would have swept away the shadowy terrors. He would have lifted us all into the daylight. But, alas, he was I knew not where; and his name was never mentioned in the hearing of Lord and Lady St. Leger.

Then the blow fell. One afternoon Garret Dawson had been to see my grandfather and talked with him alone; and at dinner my grandmother's face bore traces of tears, and I noticed that my grandfather's hand shook so that he spilt his wine. There was not a word spoken, and after a time the silence got on my nerves, so that I began to dread I knew not what, and could almost have burst into tears from the tension.

We had dined where we often dined when we were alone, in a little room, panelled with black oak, which opens off the hall. It is bright enough when a fire leaps and sparkles in the grate, but it was then too warm for fires, and the room seemed cheerless even while the white cloth was on the table and the lit candles made the silver and glass sparkle.

And presently, when Neil Doherty had taken away the cloth and we sat around the polished black table with nothing on it but a couple of candles and a decanter of port wine and glasses, the room looked very sad.

My grandfather tapped with his hand on the table, a thing I have known him to do when in trouble, and again the tears overflowed my grandmother's eyes and ran down her cheeks. And I felt that something was coming.

Then my grandfather cleared his throat, and leaning his face in his hand so that I should not see it, he said—

"There is something that concerns you, Bawn, which I wish to lay before you. You have been a good child always, kind and obedient to us. And now it is in your power to do more for us than ever you have done before."

He paused, and in the silence I heard the rain falling on the gravel path. It had been threatening all the afternoon. The wind soughed; it was going to be a wild night.

"Mr. Dawson has been with me this afternoon," he went on. "We talked of you, Bawn. Bawn, child, Richard Dawson wishes to marry you. Can you marry him, Bawn? If you can do it Garret Dawson gives up to me on your wedding-day certain documents which hold in them the disgrace of our family. We are old, Bawn, and we have loved you and been good to you. There are some things we could not bear. Child, can you say 'Yes?'"

I felt now as though I had known it all the time. I had a queer memory of a room in which a man lay imprisoned, the walls of which came closer and closer every day till they should press him to death. It was a tale I had read somewhere. So this had been closing in on me all those months. I was to marry Richard Dawson, I who loved Anthony Cardew with all my heart and soul.

CHAPTER XXV

THE LOVER

"And Theobald," I asked, after that pause—"what about Theobald?"

"Theobald is young. He has a thousand chances of happiness," answered my grandfather, somewhat eagerly. "If he could know he would be the first to sacrifice himself to prevent the disgrace. I tell you, Bawn, that if Garret Dawson publishes the secret he holds it will kill your grandmother and me as surely as though he had shot us through the heart. Child, child, we would have given you the world if we could! Can you do this much for us?"

I looked at his poor old, twitching, grey face, at his hands that worked pitifully. I saw my grandmother lift her streaming eyes to Heaven as though to ask for help. They had been very tender to me, and they were old. God knows no woman ever shrank more from a lover than I from Richard Dawson. But, perhaps, if I sacrificed myself, following the example of our Lord himself, He would take me away from the intolerable marriage. He would let me save them, and then He would take me to himself.

"I will marry Richard Dawson," I said quietly.

I saw an immense relief in the poor old faces, although their cloud barely lifted. They did not thank me. Perhaps they knew I could not have borne it. I saw them creep closer together as though for comfort, as I got up and went away to my own room.

I was as glad as I could be of anything that Nora had gone a day or two earlier to nurse one of her uncle's children who was sick. How could I have borne her presence about me? To think I had saved her and had myself fallen into the net! And at least she had loved the man, incredible as it seemed, while I recoiled from him with loathing, because I loved another man with my whole heart and soul.

Something within me cried out that it would be a wicked marriage. I fell on my knees by my bed, but I could not pray. I felt numb and sick. I stretched my arms out across the little white bed where I had slept so happily, despite the ghosts. I laid my face upon them and stayed there in a trance of misery.

I heard my grandmother pause at the door and listen as she went down the corridor to her bedroom, and I dreaded that she should come in; but, perhaps, thinking from the silence that I was asleep she went on after the pause.

I must have fallen asleep in that comfortless position for when I awoke I was chilled and stiff. There was white moonlight in the room, and I heard, with a sinking of my heart, the crying of the woman in the shrubbery. She always came when there was trouble. Well, God knows, there was trouble enough now, such a coil of trouble for me that death had been an easy way out of it.

I crept into bed and thought miserably of what Anthony Cardew would think of me when he should hear of my disgrace. Of course he would not know why I had married Richard Dawson. He had yielded me up to poor Theobald as he thought, and instead of Theobald, whom I might have loved if I had never seen Anthony Cardew, handsome, generous, of honourable lineage, he would know that I had married Richard Dawson, with his bad traditions behind him, and himself a wild, careless liver, with many sins to his account. He would never know how I loathed it. Perhaps he would even think that I married for money. Even if I were dead, and I felt I must die of marrying Richard Dawson, he could never think of me except with contempt and loathing.

The next morning Maureen came with my tea.

"Why are you looking like alabaster on your pillow?" she asked, with some indignation. "There's good news coming, I tell you. There's good news coming. See how fine the morning is! I never slept a sweeter sleep, and it was in my sleep I had word."

I shrank even from Maureen's half-mad eyes. What would she say when she knew that I was to marry Richard Dawson? She had always loved Theobald and had looked forward to our marriage. I was afraid of Maureen's eyes.

"I'll toss the cup for you," she said when I had drunk my tea. "There's a beautiful fortune in it for you, Miss Bawn. I see a wedding-coach and four horses—"

"Are there plumes on the coach, Maureen?" I asked.

"I'm surprised at you, Miss Bawn." Maureen looked startled and angry. "Why should there be plumes on the wedding-coach that'll bring yourself and the fine husband home? I won't be asking who he'll be. And by-and-by there'll be babies in the nurseries again, and old Maureen'll be as young as ever she was."

The afternoon of that day I was called down to Richard Dawson, and when I went to the drawing-room I found him alone.

He took me in his arms and kissed me, and when I shivered under his kiss it only seemed to make him more ardent. It was a terrible thing to accept his kisses feeling that cold repulsion; and my whole heart and soul another man's. If he had been less ardent it might have been more tolerable. As it was I let him have his will of kissing me till he suddenly put me away from him.

"You do not return my kisses," he said. "Are you afraid of me, Bawn?"

"I am not used to lovers," I said, turning away my head.

"Ah, I frightened you that day in the wood, my bird," he said, "and I suffer for it now. What a brute I was! But you can make me different if you will, Bawn. If you will but love me, my beauty, you can do what you will with me, make a decent fellow of me. I am not such a bad fellow at heart. Come, give me a kiss of your own free will. You would not when I asked you before, but you will now because I am your affianced husband. Come, kiss me, Bawn."

I kissed him, shrinking all the time, and with a dreary wonder as to whether it was always going to be like this, and if so, how I was to endure it.

"Your kiss is as cold as a frog," he said. "But never mind, I wouldn't give a fig for a woman who was too easily won. The time will come when you will beg me for kisses. Till then, why, I shall do the love-making myself."

But presently, seeing I could not endure it, he let me go. It never seemed to occur to him that my aversion could be for him. He took my shrinking as maiden modesty, and vowed that he delighted in it, that I should have been far less desirable if I had not been so coy, and that he would be happier breaking down my barriers than if there had been none to break.

Finally he took a little case from his pocket, and out of it he produced a ring, the beauty of which would have delighted any happy girl. It was set with an emerald of great size and beauty, of a heart-shape, surrounded by diamonds, and at the top a true-lovers' knot in diamonds. He put it on my finger, saying that he had carried it about with him for a month or more, and that he had paid a pretty price for it. It was an antique ring and the workmanship very beautiful, not like those made nowadays.

It occurred to me that he had been very sure of me. But I said nothing while he put on the ring.

"And how soon will you marry me, Bawn?" he asked. "There is nothing I will not give you when we are married. I am going to take you away and show you the beautiful world. There will be nothing you can desire that will not be yours. Oh, you shall see what a lover I will make! Bawn, Bawn, you will adore me."

"It is too soon to talk of wedding-days," I said.

"Not too soon for me," he answered. "I can hardly bear to wait. I would marry you this instant if I could. Will it be in a month's time, Bawn?"

"I could never be ready," I said.

"Not in a month's time! And how do you suppose I am going to endure even that! I shall talk to Lady St. Leger about it. She will be merciful to me."

"I could not be ready," I said. "Not under two months. People are not married in such a hurry. There are so many things to see to."

It was only now that he began to talk of the wedding that I realized how, somewhere at the back of all the misery and shame, I had had a wild hope that Heaven might intervene and save me from the marriage. I had not thought he would be in such a hurry, that he would give me no loophole of escape. I could have cried out for a long day like any poor wretch condemned to the gallows.

"Don't you see that I am not ready? I am not used to lovers," I cried, bursting into a paroxysm of tears, when he went on urging a speedy marriage.

At the sight of my tears he seemed dismayed and tried to comfort me, saying that I should have my own time and that I was the more desirable to him because I was not ready to fall into his arms.

CHAPTER XXVI

THE TRIBUNAL

After that day there was not a day but rich presents were showered on me by the Dawsons, which reminded me of the decking of a victim led to the sacrifice.

What did I care about the jewels and furs and laces that my bridegroom brought me? About his promise of what he should give me when I was his?

Garret Dawson used to eye me with a grim approval: and I heard him say to my grandfather once that he could have had rank and wealth and beauty for his son, and that I would bring him nothing; but that he and Rick knew a unique thing when they saw it and were prepared to pay any price for it. At which speech my poor grandfather bowed with a look as though he felt it hard to endure.

Mrs. Dawson took me in her kind, old, motherly arms when she came to see me, and said humbly that she could never be grateful enough to me for consenting to marry her son; and what she said afterwards had something significant in it if I had not been too miserable to notice it.

"He'll make you a good husband, dear," she said. "He's a good boy at heart, although he has been a bit wild. And, listen, dear, you may have your feelings about the way Dawson made his money and I'm not saying you wouldn't be right. But, my dear, there's many a thing Dawson did, hard and cruel things, you understand, dear, that Rick never knew of. The love of money's not in him any more than it's in me; and he has done many a kind thing."

I was able to return the poor soul's kiss because I liked her, and always shall, and was sorry for her.

Indeed, I wanted new friends, for the old were angry with me or held aloof from me.

When my engagement was announced my godmother had come in hot haste from her cousin's dying bed, which now she hardly left, to remonstrate with my grandfather and grandmother. She had urged and pleaded with them, had done all she could, seeing that she was, as she said to me, desperately sorry for them, and had finally left them in a coldness.

"You poor child!" she said to me when I met her in the avenue, she driving her fast mare in the smart dog-cart which was her favourite equipage, I on foot. She jumped down and held the reins over her arm while she talked. "What a face for a bride! Why, Bawn, you are older by ten years than the child I used to know. They are mad, mad, poor dear souls, to let Garret Dawson frighten them; and I am helpless, because they will tell me nothing. Couldn't you stand out, Bawn?"

I shook my head.

"If only Theobald were here!" she said, in a helpless passion. "If only Theobald were here! To think that they should rob him of his sweetheart because they are caught in Dawson's spider's web. Their own grandchild! It seems unnatural. And you two lovers from your cradles!"

I don't know what impelled me to tell her the truth, but the words came to my lips and I spoke them.

"I never loved Theobald and he never loved me," I said. "They have not that at their doors. I should not have married Theobald."

"Why, God bless me, child!" she said, staring at me. "You will be telling me next that you are in love with Richard Dawson. But I shall not believe it, not with that face."

She went away with a look of hopeless bewilderment.

I fared less well with Maureen, who was bitterly angry with me and said things to me that I could not have borne if she had been always responsible for what she said.

"A fine husband you'll be getting, Miss Bawn," she said. "There's no accounting for ladies' tastes, and by all accounts there are a good many ladies who are fond of Master Richard. Ask Lady Ardaragh. There isn't much she wouldn't give him, they say. If half the stories are true, there are many that have a better right to him than you, Miss Bawn. And to think you've thrown over my darling boy for Garret Dawson's son!"

I must have looked frightened, for she became suddenly contrite, and, throwing her arms about me, rated herself for the things she had said, saying that she knew I wasn't to blame, and that it was only her love for me and Theobald which made her so bitter.

Then her mood changed; and snatching up my hand with Richard Dawson's ring on it she burst into a harsh laugh.

"What was over him at all," she said, "to give you the like o' that? Didn't he know the green was unlucky? Sure, 'tis unlucky for him it'll be, and you'll never marry him. My dream'll come true, and you'll be saved in time, Miss Bawn. The ill luck is for him, not for you."

Indeed, I found it hard in those days to meet the eyes of the neighbours, gentle and simple, who could not know why I had consented to marry Richard Dawson. I felt that the county buzzed with it, castle and cabin alike, and it made me shrink away from those who had always been kind to me. I was ashamed to go down the village street, for I knew the people would come to their doors and look after me, and say, "Isn't it a wonder for Miss Bawn that she'd marry a Dawson? and the family always so proud, too."

I noticed that none of the people who came to call were effusive in their congratulations except Lady Ardaragh, and she congratulated me with a high colour and an exaggeration of speech which did not ring true.

The Misses Chenevix called one day, and, while Miss Henrietta sat unhappily looking down at her lap, Miss Bride congratulated me in a voice which had no congratulation in it.

"I wish you happiness, Bawn," she said. "Not that I ever think marriage a subject for congratulation, but rather for condolence."

A somewhat dreary sense of the humour of the speech made me answer that I thought I agreed with her, whereupon she snapped me up and said that, to be sure, some people must be married, though she for her part thought the world would get on very well without marriage; but then, of course, she was old-fashioned.

"And if you had to marry, Bawn," she went on, "why didn't you wait for your cousin? The county always expected you to marry your cousin; and, if you must be married, Theobald would have suited you better than Mr. Dawson. You're not the girl I thought you, Bawn."

I wondered what Theobald would think of me. I had left it to my grandparents to explain to Theobald, and his letters to me had gone unanswered now for three weeks or more.

But, after all, it was not Theobald who was my tribunal; it was not from Theobald's judgment I shrank.

It was Anthony Cardew I feared most. When I endured the ignominy of Richard Dawson's kisses, when he would hold me in his arms with his face against mine and I felt that nothing worse could happen to me, I used to keep wondering all the time what Anthony Cardew would think of me when he knew.

The thought made me desperate. I could have slit my nose and chin, defaced myself like St. Ursula and her maidens, so that I should cease to be desirable to Richard Dawson. But there were my grandparents, and the disgrace which I must buy back for them by giving myself.

Then one day, being in great misery, it occurred to me that I would write a letter to Anthony Cardew. I was quite sure that I should be dead before he received it, for I knew I should not live long with Richard Dawson as his wife, if indeed I were not saved before that. I was glad to think that I was growing thin; that I was languid on the least exertion, and had no appetite for my food. I hoped that God would be merciful to me, and that I should just save them and die. And presently Theobald would come home to them and they would be happy.

And so I thought that I would write a letter to Anthony Cardew, so that when I was dead he would understand and be sorry for me. And I sat down and wrote it. For I could not bear that he should think me unworthy and shameful, seeing that I loved him with all my heart and soul.

CHAPTER XXVII

BROSNA

I made several attempts at the letter, and discarded them all. And at last, lest I should be interrupted and the letter never be written, I wrote in a great hurry.

"Dear Captain Cardew,

"I hope this letter will reach you safely, so that in the days to come you will not misjudge me. You wrote to me that you were giving me up to my cousin. That you could not do, for I loved only you, and did from the hour I first laid eyes on you, and shall forever. But, loving you, I am going to marry Richard Dawson, the money-lender's son. And I must tell you, lest you should misjudge me, and all women for my sake, that I shall marry him most unwillingly. I do it because Garret Dawson holds a secret of ours which only the sacrifice of myself can buy back. I owe so much to the kind love which has never let me miss the love of father and mother. But I am sure I shall not live long. You should not have gone away and left me.

"Yours always,
"BAWN."

When I had written it I did not read it over, lest I should destroy it with the others, but, having found a very strong envelope, I put it within it and sealed it with the impression of my father's ring.

The only way I could hope for it to reach him was by leaving it at his old home, which I knew he loved despite its state of ruin, or perhaps the more because of that, and he was sure to return there some time. So I addressed it to Captain Cardew, Brosna; and then, because I could trust no one but myself to deliver it I stole out of the house.

I was free for a few hours, for my lover was gone to Dublin. He had taken a cottage in the neighbourhood, because he had once heard me express a liking for it. It was a pretty little place, enclosed by high walls which held within them many beauties. It would have been an exquisite place for a pair of happy lovers; and he was making it very fine and dainty for me. It had been unoccupied for some years; and he was having it newly decorated and furnishing it with the prettiest things money could buy. He had said that I was not to see it till it was ready for me; and it occupied as much of his time as he could spare from me. In Dublin he was picking up all manner of pretty things in the way of antique furniture and china and glass and silver and pictures. We were to stay at the cottage a few days after our marriage, before we went abroad; and afterwards it was to be our home till such time as I desired a finer one.

He was so generous that at times I felt ashamed that he should do so much for an unwilling bride; and if I could have felt less aversion for him I would gladly have done so. I used to feel that if I could watch him lavishing everything on another woman, for he squandered his love as well as his money on me, I could have liked and admired him.

The woods were full of the yellow leaves of autumn and the wind sighed mournfully in the bare branches as I went on my way to the postern in the wall. Outside it I turned to the left, and walked for half a mile or so along a grassy road, overhung with trees, till I came to the entrance gates of Brosna.

The lodge was empty, and the gate yielded to a push. There was an air of neglect about everything that was very sad. Part of one of the pillars which supported the entrance gate was down. In the avenue some trees that had fallen last winter lay across the way; no one had troubled to remove them.

I knew there was no one in the house but Captain Cardew's soldier-servant, Terence Murphy, whose old mother lived in Araglin village. I did not want to meet Terence; and I had an idea, having heard of the great extent of Brosna, indeed, it was easy to judge of it from the aspect of the place outside, that I might slip in somewhere and leave my letter without meeting with him.

So, without going near the hall door, I passed through a little iron gate in the wall at one end of the house, which I found led to an overgrown garden.

The grass in the garden was as high as my waist, and here and there a rose tree, standing up above the tangle, showed a pale autumn rose; and little old-fashioned chrysanthemum bushes bore their clusters of tawny and lilac flowers. Beyond, I could see a kitchen garden with the apples in the boughs, and, standing up in the midst of it, a projecting part of the house which, to my amazement, was covered with thatch.

I was reassured at the moment by hearing Terence Murphy's voice shouting at a distance. It must have been at the other side of the house, in the stable-yard, I judged, and I thought I should be able to deliver my letter before he could by any possibility reach where I was.

There was a glass door leading from the thatched room into the garden, and I found that it stood open. I noticed that in front of it the grass plot had been cleared and there were flowers in the borders. Within I found a very pretty and comfortable room arranged with unexpected tidiness. As I looked about me I remembered having heard that Terence always kept a place in readiness for the return of his master. All the rest of the place might be in ruin, but this room was pleasant and home-like.

It had once been a woman's room, I thought, from certain prettinesses, the blue, rose-wreathed carpet on the floor, the ceiling groined under its thatch and painted in blue with a crescent moon and stars in gold, the walls covered with silk set in panels.

But now it was a man's room, with the pleasant litter of a man's belongings. There was a square writing-table in the window, with a wooden chair drawn up in front of it. There were many pipes, old and new, and whips and hunting-crops; and a gun-case standing by the wall and some crossed weapons on the wall. I saw a pair of spurs in one corner, and, flung carelessly on the writing-table, as though the owner might return at any moment, there was a glove.

I took up the glove and kissed it furtively. I wished I might have taken it to comfort me, for a sense of the hand it had held seemed to linger about it. As I stood pressing it to my breast my eye fell on a picture that stood on the writing-table, a picture that was like yet unlike myself. It was a reproduction of the miniature I remembered.

There were other pictures and photographs about—men in uniform, women of many ages, horses and dogs: one of Anthony Cardew himself, which made my heart beat to look at it. I wished I might have taken it also, and had the will to do it but I dared not. Besides, what right had I to such things? Already I was trying to steel myself to destroy the one letter he had written me. I should have no right to it when I was Richard Dawson's wife.

A shout somewhere near at hand alarmed me. I slipped my letter under the glove on the writing-table and fled out precipitately. Only in time, as it proved, for Terence Murphy came round the house chasing a refractory hen, which, as luck would have it, flew through the door I had left open behind me.

"I could have sworn I shut that door," I heard Terence shout at the top of his voice. "Bad luck to ye, ye divil"—to the hen—"God forgive me for swearing. Will nothin' contint ye but the master's own room?"

While he dived within the room I got out through the little gate and back into the avenue, where the briars and undergrowth had made hedges behind which one could easily find cover.

Once in safety I stopped to gaze back at the long front of Brosna, looking so sad. It is one of the white stuccoed houses so common in Ireland in the eighteenth century, although much finer and more magnificent than most. At the roof there was a balustrading, and below were long lines of windows of a uniform oblong shape, each with an architrave above it. The rains of our moist climate had wept upon it and there were long green streaks extending down the walls. I saw now that there was a sunken storey with a sort of area that ran all round the house, so that Brosna, except for its thatched summer-room, was a house of three storeys, not of two, as it appeared at first.

While I looked at it the evening shadows crept down upon it and seemed to enfold it in a greater loneliness. But it was dearer to me than the great houses of the neighbourhood which were comfortable and well kept and inhabited. And I was glad to think of the ordered room, with its grass plot before the window, and the fire set in the grate, ready to be lit when the master should come home.

CHAPTER XXVIII

THE QUICK AND THE DEAD

When I reached home I found that my grandmother had been looking for me, and Neil Doherty told me the reason. Word had come from Castle Clody that Miss Champion's cousin was dead.

"You must go to her, Bawn," said my grandmother, sadly. "We must not leave her alone, and she will not want me. You will spend the night with her?"

Yes, I would do that, although I shrank from the prospect of death like any other sensitive girl. It was not likely I would refuse to go to my dear godmother in her hour of need; and I had an unacknowledged hope that she might keep me with her, perhaps, so that I would be free of my lover for a few days.

When she heard that I had come she came down to me where I was standing by the fire in the morning-room warming my hands, for the first frost of the season had come and the night was cold.

"Ah, good child," she said, "to come so quickly! Everything is done, Bawn, and she is at rest. I shall miss her dreadfully. I don't know what I shall do with my empty hands. I am too old to begin to love again."

Every one knew that Miss Joan had been querulous and bitter with her, and it made me love and reverence her more than ever to hear the way she spoke.

"Sit down, Bawn," she said, "sit down. You are going to stay with me, kind child. I shall have the little room off my own prepared for you; and we shall have our dinner here. It will be more cheerful than in the dining-room."

I could not help noticing that though her eyes showed traces of much weeping she yet wore a singularly tranquil and even radiant look, as though good news had come to her. Indeed, the whole atmosphere of the house seemed strangely peaceful.

A servant came in to set the table, and we went upstairs to the little room within her own room where I was to sleep. A bright fire already blazed in the grate, and Louise was busy putting out my things. The room looked so cheerful with its chintz, a green trellis hung with roses on a white ground, that one could not be gloomy and fearful in it, even if I did not know that my dear godmother would leave the door between our rooms open at night and would wake if I but stirred.

Louise helped me to put on the one black gown I possessed, which, as it happened, was patterned with roses, a crêpe de Chine fichu about the neck, and I asked Louise to take it off and find me something more becoming; but my godmother would have it so, saying that poor Joan would not grudge me a few roses, having herself found the roses of Paradise.

That quiet radiancy of my godmother seemed to diffuse itself over everything. I know I felt happier than I had felt for a long time, and I tried to put all the trouble, and the thought that I was to marry Richard Dawson the week before Christmas, out of my mind.

Everything about the dinner-table was so pretty. I could not help feeling that my godmother had told them it was to be so; and the wax candles shone on the scarlet berries and russet and orange and crimson leaves, on the delicate napery and glass and silver; and the fire leaped and sparkled in the grate. I had a feeling that I and my godmother were shut in together from the world's trouble, although it waited for us outside the gate.

After dinner we sat by the fire and talked in a low voice, and I could not help commenting on the new serene happiness of my godmother's face. I had always thought it a cheerful face before, although the face of one who had suffered; but now I wondered that I had thought it anything but sad.

"You look happy!" I said.

"And I am happy, Bawn, although I shall miss Joan. But she is at rest with God, and before she died she told me something which set my heart at rest."

"Ah, I am glad of that," I said.

She leant forward and took my hands in hers, making me turn round so as to face her.

"Bawn," she said, "there is nothing worth having in the world but love, nothing but love, nothing but love. I tell it to you, although some people would think that love had wrecked my life. But I have loved greatly, and I have been loved greatly, and I would not change places with any of your wives and mothers of families."

"Yes, I know," I said.

"And if you do, Bawn, why don't you save yourself from this marriage? The money doesn't tempt you, nor Richard Dawson's coarse comeliness. Why don't you save yourself, child?"

I shook my head helplessly.

"If it were anything in which money could help I would sell all I have rather than see you marry without love."

"Money has nothing to do with it. And—it is too late to do anything."

"It would never be too late so long as you were not his wife. They are deceived. Luke L'Estrange was the truest and most candid soul alive. Yet what a web of lies has grown up about him. Shall I tell you, Bawn, what Joan told me before she died?"

"If it eases you."

"I have to share it with someone, and I can trust you not to think hardly of my poor Joan."

I wondered what was coming, but I had not long to wait. My godmother looked at me again, straight into my eyes, as though she would see to the depths of my soul.

"I have forgiven her, poor dear soul, with all my heart," she said. "If I thought you could judge her hardly I would not tell you; but I think you will not judge her hardly. You see, she loved Luke. He had a way with women. She was always delicate and sickly, and he was sorry for her. He used to sit by her and talk to her. She loved him and she thought that he loved her, or would love her if I were out of the way. I had everything, she thought—health and wealth and the world before me, and Luke's love. She thought it unfair that I should have so much. No wonder she wanted Luke for herself."

Again her eyes looked into mine, asking a question. Whatever she saw satisfied her, for she went on again with dreamy tenderness—

"I see you can pity her, Bawn. Child, how do you know it if you never loved? He came to this house when he was flying from justice, as he thought, expecting to find me and found her instead. He gave her such messages for me as might make any woman proud. He would release me, but he knew I was too great-hearted to accept the release; he had killed Jasper Tuite in the struggle when he tried to save Irene Cardew from him. He had seen Jasper Tuite strike poor Irene when he was trying to drag her from her carriage to ride with him on his horse. She was screaming, poor girl, and Jasper Tuite struck her on the mouth. And what would my Luke do save spring on to Jasper Tuite and close with him? And Jasper Tuite would have shot him if Luke had not fired in self-defence. No jury would have convicted Luke, for Jasper Tuite died from heart-failure, not from the flesh-wound of Luke's pistol. But if I had only been here when he stole here under cover of the darkness I would have made him hold his ground."

"And he saw Miss Standish instead?"

"Yes, he saw Joan. And she kept his messages all these years. There was more than that. I was to send him a message to where he was in hiding, waiting for a passage to America. I sent him none, but Joan sent him one instead. She was jealous, terribly jealous, or she could not have done it, poor girl. She sent him word that he was not to return, that Jasper Tuite was dead of his wound. Also she sent him word from me that I wanted no more of him. How could he have believed it? Well, the remorse of it has gone far to kill her. If she was ever trying, it was because she had to take benefits from the woman she had wronged. Poor unhappy Joan! She died in great love and peace with me."

Fortunately, this time she did not look me in the eyes. Such magnanimity was beyond me.

"It is very sweet to know," she went on dreamily, "that poor Luke came to me in his need. He knew he could trust my love. But he ought to have known me better than to believe I could send that message. He ought to have known me better."

"Yes," I said, "he ought to have known you better."

CHAPTER XXIX

THE SICKNESS

It was while I was still at Castle Clody that a message came to me one morning saying that some one desired to speak with me; and when I went out into the hall I found it was Nora Brady. She had a little crimson shawl over her head, and as she lifted her eyes to me her beauty came to me like a new thing. There was dry snow in the wind, and a few flakes of it showed on her dark curls, which lay ring on ring under the shawl. Her face was round and soft as a child's, and the innocence of her blue, black-lashed eyes as she lifted them to me was as unsullied as though she were three years old. She had lost her pretty colour, but the gentleness which made her beauty appealing was, if possible, greater than of old.

"You wanted to speak to me, Nora," I said.

I know I turned red and pale when her eyes met mine; for the moment all social differences and distinctions ceased to be. I was going to marry the man Nora loved, the man I loathed. I had a feeling that it was an intolerable wrong.

"If you please, Miss Bawn," she said.

The servants were passing up and down the staircase. I did not want any witnesses to our interview, nor any eavesdroppers.

"Come in here, Nora," I said, opening the door of the morning-room which I usually had to myself for an hour or so after breakfast. "And how is the child? Better, I hope."

"Little Katty is quite well again, Miss Bawn, and I've come to tell you, please Miss Bawn, that I'd rather not come back. 'Tisn't that I'm ungrateful, Miss. No young lady could be kinder and better than you. But my uncle is going to marry again, and if you please, Miss Bawn, I think I should like to go to America."

"Don't go to America, Nora," I said; "it's a terrible place. I'll look after you. I'll speak to Miss Champion, and we'll see what we can do. Miss Champion has so many friends. She'll easily get you another place, away from this, in Dublin."

Suddenly the large tears filled Nora's eyes and trickled down her cheeks. She wept in rivers as a child does, and as painlessly.

"Don't ask me to stay, Miss Bawn," she said brokenly. "I want to put the ocean between me and him. I've done my best to pull him up out of my heart, and I've prayed my best, but I go on caring for him still. I'd better be away, Miss Bawn."

"Very well, Nora," I said, in a miserable perplexity. If she cared for Richard Dawson so much it was she who ought to marry him, peasant girl as she was. It was a shame that I should step into her place, loathing it. "Very well," I said. "I will do what I can to help you. When do you go, Nora?"

"Not till after Christmas, Miss. There won't be any emigration till the worst of the winter storms are over. Thank you kindly, Miss Bawn, but I don't think there's anything you can do for me. The nuns'll find me an employment while I stay. You're not vexed with me for leaving, Miss Bawn?"

"No, Nora, I quite understand," I said. And then on an impulse I kissed her.

I knew she was fond of me, almost as fond as my old dog; and she did not hate me, although I was going to marry the man she loved. She flushed when I kissed her, and the tears came again to her eyes.

"You are very good to me, Miss Bawn," she said. "Not many ladies would be so good to a poor girl. I hope you'll be happy, Miss Bawn. And I hope you'll make him happy. Don't believe anything the people say about him. He has a good heart, like his mother. He's been good to me. Sure, if he wasn't strong for the two of us, I'd have had no stren'th at all, though I promised you, Miss Bawn. Many a day when I sat by little Katty, and the other children were at school and the place quiet I thought I'd have to run out of it to him. Maybe I'd have done it too, only I knew it was no use, because you had his heart."

She went a little way towards the door. Then she came back again.

"I wouldn't be goin' too much to Araglin, Miss Bawn, if I was you," she said. "There's a deal of sickness there. You wouldn't know what it might be going to be."

Somehow this thought of hers for me touched me more than anything else.

"I'll keep away, Nora," I said, "unless it might be that I ought to go. We weren't afraid of the famine fever in the old times. If there were to be such a thing again we might have to do what we did then."

"Ye died with the people then," she said, pausing with her hand on the door-handle. "But sure, why would there be the fever? Isn't there as fine a crop as ever was seen of potatoes? And Master Richard wouldn't let you put a hair of your head in danger. I'm not sayin' there's anything in the sickness. It's a sick time o' year. But if there was anything you should keep away, Miss Bawn. There's lots to do it without you. You're not looking too well now. Master Richard should be uneasy for you."

I spoke to my godmother about Nora later in the day, keeping back her secret, but only telling her that there were reasons which made her feel she must go. She knew the girl, was interested in her, and as it happened, one of her many friends had written to her that she wanted a young maid to be with two little girls. The situation was in England. Perhaps Nora would be satisfied if the Irish Sea lay between her and Richard Dawson.

I was returning home in the afternoon of the next day. My lover was restive over the loss of so much of my society. But the morning was bright and cheerful, and I thought I would walk over to Araglin and lay the matter before Nora.

It was a most delightful autumn day. There had been a hoar-frost in the night and the dead leaves and twigs had a tracery of silver and crackled under one's foot as one walked. It was a day for exhilaration if one were happy, and, despite the load of care which hung heavy upon me, I found myself walking less languidly than I had done of late. The boughs were now all bare; and where one had only seen leaves one saw a network of trees and branches against a blue sky, and beyond the trees the Purple Hill, which is hidden from one on our tree-hung road so long as the trees are in leaf. The little robins sang cheerfully in many trees, and the air was so still that a beech-nut falling from the tree made quite a great noise.

As I came down the hilly road to where the village smoked in its hollow, I had an idea that a stillness lay upon it like the blue mists of autumn that were over all the countryside. Araglin is usually the noisiest of villages; cocks crowing, hens cackling, dogs barking, children shouting at their play. But this morning it was silent.

Nora's uncle's house lay almost outside the village, quite at its beginning. I thought I should find her there alone, but, as it happened, when I was close to it, she came out carrying a pail, evidently on her way to fetch water from a stream which flowed by the roadside and here and there widened into a little well.

She was close to me before she saw me. When she did at last catch sight of me I was amazed at the swift change in the expression of her face. It had been moody enough when I had had time to observe it in repose. Now something of fear, of horror, leaped into it.

"Go back at once, Miss Bawn, for God's sake!" she cried. "Go back, and don't be coming near me. There's small-pox in the village and I've been in and out with them. Half the village is sickening for it; the doctor's distracted. He's sent word up to Dublin to send nurses and doctors. Thank God, I was able to turn you back. Go home, Miss Bawn, and come here no more."

"And what are you going to do, Nora?" I asked.

"Is it me, Miss Bawn? Sure, I'll stay where I am. I've been in and out with them; and if I'm to get it, I'll get it. Ask someone to take the children away. Then I'll be able to help with the nursing. Maybe 'tis what God meant for me."

We stood and looked at each other across the space. Why, it was what I had desired, that my face should be marred, so that Richard Dawson would turn away from me in disgust. For a moment I had an impulse to cross the line she had set for me, to go as she had gone into infected places. Perhaps she read the thought in my face, for she cried out to me to go away, to remember those who depended on me for happiness and go. She wrung her hands when I did not go.

"Go away, for God's sake," she cried again, "and don't have the face he cares about destroyed with the small-pox! See now, Miss Bawn, darling, what would his Lordship and her Ladyship do without you?"

But while she coaxed me with their names I could see that she dreaded the small-pox for me lest my face should be spoilt for Richard Dawson, and I thought it one of the greatest things I had known in the heart of a woman.

CHAPTER XXX

THE DARK DAYS

I remember the weeks after that like a bad dream. The small-pox had spread from Araglin to other villages and to the isolated cabins. No one knew where it had come from, or where it would go next, for it spread like wildfire. And the doctors and nurses had come down from Dublin in a cheerful little band and were fighting it heroically. For some weeks there were only new outbreaks to tell of. For some weeks there were panic and terror everywhere.

My lover wanted to marry me and carry me away out of the danger; but that I would not hear of. It was enough that to please him I must shut myself away in a selfish isolation. If I had been a free woman I would have insisted on going, as my godmother had gone, while yet the help was wanted. During those weeks I was cut off from the comfort of her presence, for even when she was no longer needed she was in quarantine lest she should have taken the infection.

I will say that the Dawsons gave generously of their money for the aid of the people.

When we knew first of the outbreak and heard that Mary Champion was in the thick of it, my lover was moody and silent for a while even when he was with me.

I remember once that he kicked at a coal which had fallen from the fire and lay on the hearth, and he frowned heavily.

"I ought to have been there, Bawn," he said, "and it isn't that I was afraid. Good Lord! I should think not. You would like me just as well with my beauty spoilt in such a cause. But it is that you make a coward of me, little girl. When I think that anything might happen now to prevent our marriage it makes me sweat with fear. Else I would have risked my life over and over again, and not have cared two straws about it."

"I know you are brave," I said, at which he looked pleased and said that it was the first kind word I had given him.

In these days he did not force his caresses upon me as much as he did at first, but used to call me his little nun, and say in his usual boastful way that he would make me in time eager for that from which

I turned away now. Every day as our marriage came nearer I dreaded it more, and felt as if I must run away to the ends of the earth rather than endure it; but when I looked at my grandfather's face I knew there was no help for me.

The marriage was fixed for the 20th of December, and I could see that he was nearly as impatient for it as my bridegroom. I could see that on this side of my wedding-day there lay for him the chance that the disgrace might come at any moment. On the other side was peace and safety.

The fear of the secret the Dawsons held possessed him so much that he had no thought for me, as he had had none for Theobald while he still believed that there was some sort of engagement between Theobald and me.

I confessed I had dreaded what Theobald would think of my marriage, not knowing the reason of it. But my anxieties on that score were set at rest, for, as soon as possible after he had heard of the engagement, he wrote a most affectionate letter to me. I could read in its effusiveness that he was so relieved to know of my marriage that he was not disposed to be critical over my bridegroom. He sent me a present of a rug of leopard skins and some fine pieces of wrought silver work, and in a postscript he mentioned that there was someone he wanted us to welcome presently, a Miss Travers, a beauty—young, good, gifted, an heiress.

"She would be the same to me," he added in his round, schoolboy handwriting, "if she hadn't a penny; but I am glad for the sake of Aghadoe that she has money. Dear Bawn, I adore her."

I had guessed it all the time, and remembered that he had mentioned Miss Travers before, and that the manner of it was significant. Dear Theobald, it was easy enough to see through his simple guile!

My grandparents, having ascertained that Miss Travers was a quite unexceptional person, had an access of cheerfulness. I could see that once I was married and the paper in their hands, whatever it was, they would begin to look forward to Theobald's return and his marriage. There would be great days at Aghadoe yet; but I should not be there to see them.

When I came to be measured for my wedding-dress my grandmother discovered how thin I had become.

"You will be all right," she said, "when Richard carries you away from this sad and troubled country to the south and to the sun."

Long before this my lover had taken the alarm and fretted over me with anxious tenderness, saying that they had not known how to take care of me, and that once I was his I should be taken care of as no other woman ever was before.

Fortunately for him he was much at the Cottage in those days, superintending the last arrangements, else I think, ardent as he was, he could hardly have borne with me, for I was alternately listless and bitter, so that I have seen my dear old grandmother look at me in sad wonder; and that always reduced me to repentance.

As the time of my marriage came nearer I felt the ignominy the more. I used to think that the very portraits on the walls looked at me askance because I was going to marry the usurer's son. I was sure the old servants were not the same, any more than the old friends; but, oddly enough, Maureen had forgiven me, had held me to her breast and cried over me. I felt that she knew the marriage would kill me, she only of them all. Every night now the ghosts cried as they had cried when I was a child, when Uncle Luke went away.

It might have been a week from my wedding-day when there lay one morning beside my plate a letter, the handwriting on which made my heart leap up.

Fortunately I was first at the table and I was able to hide the letter. I could not have read it under the eyes of my grandparents, and they must have noticed if I had taken it away unopened, because I had so few correspondents, apart from the wedding-presents and congratulations.

I had barely hidden it when my grandparents took their places, and Neil Doherty set the big Crown Derby teapot before my grandmother and then went round and removed the cover of the silver dish that was in front of my grandfather. I believe the three of us between us did not eat the food of one healthy appetite in those days; but the things appeared all the same, and hot dishes were flanked by cold meats on the side-board as though we had the appetites of hunters.

I heard Neil say as he stood by my grandfather that, glory be to God, the sickness was disappearing, that there hadn't been a new case in Araglin village for more than a fortnight, and the doctors thought that the worst was over. Our servants were on the usual terms of Irish servants with their employers, that is to say, they treated us with a respectful familiarity; and now that owing to the sickness there was little visiting we had to depend upon Neil mostly for our news.

"It will not be the same at Miss Bawn's wedding, Neil," I heard my grandfather say, "as though there had not been the sickness. When I married her Ladyship the whole county came to see it."

"True for you," said Neil. "There's many a one under the sod that looked to dance at Miss Bawn's wedding, and there's many another that their own mothers won't know when they see them."

"The great thing is," said my grandmother, "that the sickness is coming to an end. Please God, we can lift up our hearts towards the New Year."

"And thank God for that," said my grandfather; and I felt that it was not only for cessation of the sickness he gave thanks.

There were, indeed, many new graves, and many, too, whose living or dying yet hung in the balance; and if I had been a happy woman I would have felt it ominous to be married at such a time. But as it was, nothing mattered.

"You are sure Nora Brady has not taken the sickness, Neil?" I asked.

"No, Miss Bawn; she's safe so far. To be sure, she might be inkybatin' it"—Neil, like all our people, loves a long word—"and she'll have to put up a month's quarentine when the last o' the sickness is over. I hear she's been everywhere it was."

After breakfast I escaped to the summer-house in the shrubbery with my letter. The first snow lay on the ground and was white on the dark, shining leaves of the laurels and laurestinus, but my hands trembled and burned as I opened the letter. Why did he write to me now when I had become used to my misery? As the sheet rustled in my hands I felt such a longing and a desire for him that if he called me across the world I must go.

CHAPTER XXXI

THE WEDDING DRESS

"My dear," the letter began, "I have your letter. Most happily my rascal, Terence, forwarded it; most happily, and by the grace of God, as I think, I thought to leave him the name of a halting-place where I might pick up letters, yet I expected none. What a dullard I was, Bawn, not to have known! I compared my years and sorrows and my white hairs with your youth and beauty, and I thought you must love that golden lad, your cousin. Heart's delight, it will take all the years that are left to me to tell you my gratitude. There will be no sacrifice, child, and I do certainly believe there is no secret that Lord and Lady St. Leger need fear. I should come to you on the wings of the wind if there was not a reason that I must stay a little while, and if it were not that someone is hurrying to Aghadoe whom I can trust to tear the web of lies to pieces. He will come in time, and I shall not long delay to follow. And you are mine and I am yours forever and ever.

"Your devoted
"Anthony Cardew."

The letter at once delighted and bewildered me. For a while I gave myself up to the delight, kissing it and crying over it like a mad creature. Then I came back to the cold light of facts. Just four days now to elapse before my wedding-day. What could happen in those four days to save me? Anthony's messenger, nay, Anthony himself, could do nothing. There was always my grandfather's face of suspense, by which I knew he counted the hours, always my grandmother's piteous air of asking for forgiveness. Not even Anthony Cardew could absolve me from what they bound me to.

I tried to be sorry for having written him that letter. Nothing, indeed, had been farther from my thoughts than that it should be forwarded to him. He wrote from Assumption, an island in the South Seas. If he was by my side he could hardly save me, unless he could prove that Uncle Luke was innocent of the things Garret Dawson attributed to him and could prove it to the world. And how could he do that?

I had never asked what the secret was, feeling that it must be something very terrible indeed when my grandfather would not tell it to Miss Champion. I never meant to ask. Let the proof of it be given up and forgotten. There was even a certain dreary pleasure in feeling that I was going to save the Lord and Lady St. Leger from that disgrace. It was not right the old should suffer and be afraid.

At last I put the letter inside my bodice and returned to the house. I got upstairs unobserved and put it away in the tall, spindle-legged Sheraton desk which has held all my girlish treasures. I was going to destroy the two letters from Anthony Cardew presently. Then the old life would be done with indeed.

"Bless me, child," said my grandmother, coming in on me as I closed the desk, "what a colour you have! I have not seen you look so well this many a day. What have you been doing to yourself?"

"Not rouging, Gran, I assure you," I said lightly. "I have been out in the frosty air and it has made my cheeks tingle."

"Your wedding-dress has come home," she said, "and Richard is here. He wants to see you in it, Bawn."

I remembered the superstition and wondered that she should have suggested such a thing. If I had been going to marry Anthony Cardew I should have refused, but since I was going to marry Richard Dawson I was not fearful of omens.

"Very well," I said; "I shall put it on and come downstairs."

I had a young maid from Dublin, newly come to me, and she had not our superstitions, or she was too respectful to oppose her will to mine. Anyhow, she dressed me in my wedding-dress, the fine thing of white silk, veiled with my grandmother's old Limerick lace and hung with pearls. She had dressed my hair high, quickly and deftly, and when I had on my wedding-dress she threw my wedding-veil over my head and fastened it with the diamond stars which were among my lover's gifts to me. When she had dressed me she wheeled the long mirror in front of me that I might look at myself.

I was not the same girl to look on that I had been. There was a bright colour in my cheeks and my eyes were bright; but I had a swimming in my head and I felt hot and cold by turns. I saw that I was splendid, for Margaret had put on me as many as she could of the jewels with which my lover loaded me, which used to lie about so carelessly that my grandmother had rebuked me saying I should be robbed of them one of these days. I hated them as though they had been my purchase-money; and I had scandalized Margaret only the night before by letting my necklace of emeralds and diamonds fall to the floor and lie there.

As I went down the stairs I met one or two of the servants, who drew to one side to let me pass and lifted their hands in admiration. Margaret walked behind me, being fearful, I think, that in my present mood I might let the long train sweep the stairs and corridors instead of carrying it demurely over my arm.

I paused for a moment outside the drawing-room door which stood ajar, and I could hear my lover's deep voice within. Margaret let down my train for me and I went in, up the long drawing-room to where my grandmother sat in her easy-chair by the fire and Richard Dawson stood on the hearthrug with his back to it.

As I came up the room I felt again the swimming of my head and things swayed about me for an instant. Then I recovered myself.

Between the painted panels of the drawing-room at Aghadoe there are long mirrors, in the taste of the time which could imagine nothing so decorative as a mirror. In every one of them I saw myself repeated, a slight, white figure scintillating with gems.

I had thrown back my veil and I saw the proud delight in my lover's face. He advanced a step or two to meet me and I heard my grandmother say—

"What a colour you have, child, and how bright your eyes are!"

He took up my hands and lifted them to his lips. Then he cried out, and I heard his voice as though it was at a great distance.

"She is not well, Lady St. Leger," he said, and there was a sharp note of anxiety in his tone. "Her hands were icy cold and now they are hot."

At the same moment someone came into the room and to my side. It was Maureen, and I saw that she was very angry.

"I didn't believe it when that fool of a Katty told me," she said. "Whoever heard of luck comin' to a bride who wore her wedding-dress before the day? It only needs now for Miss Bawn to go runnin' back for something after she leaves the house a bride. Sure, isn't there misfortune enough without bringin' it on us? Come along with me, my darlin' lamb, and let me get it off you. 'Tis in a fever you are this minute."

Then suddenly I lost consciousness of everything, and would have fallen on the floor in a faint if my lover had not caught me in his arms.

The next thing I knew was that the window-panes were showing themselves as lighted squares in a grey, misty world, and I could hear that somebody was speaking and what was said, even before I was awake.

"I've seen it comin' this long time," said a bitter, querulous voice that was Maureen's. "She'll go through with it, but it'll be the death of her, my darling jewel. If she's married before Master Luke comes, then he'll come too late, after all."

"Haven't I suffered enough, Maureen?" my grandmother asked pitifully—"having lost my one boy, and now to see this child slipping away from me! And there's a change in Lord St. Leger; there is, indeed, Maureen. Am I to lose them all, all?"

"Whisht, honey, whisht!" Maureen said, with sudden relenting in her voice. "God's good. Sure, He wouldn't be so hard on you as to take his Lordship, not at least till Master Luke comes home."

"And that will never be," my grandmother went on. "I've given up hope, Maureen. Luke is dead and gone, and my husband is slipping out of life, and this child is breaking her heart."

And then I opened my eyes, and they saw I was awake.

CHAPTER XXXII

THE NEW HOME

I had frightened them all by my fainting-fit, but after all it was nothing. The doctor who had been fetched hastily by my frightened lover reassured them.

"Did you think she was sickening for the small-pox?" he asked, looking from one face to the other with bright intelligence. He was a young doctor not long settled in our neighbourhood, and we used to say among ourselves that he was too clever to stay long with us. "Well, then, she isn't doing anything of the sort. I expect she's been taking the troubles too much to heart. A bit run down and nervous. The honeymoon journey will be the best prescription for that. I should like to see more flesh on her bones."

He patted my hand as he spoke; and I could see the relief in the faces about me. In those days any feverish attack suggested the small-pox.

"Dr. Molyneux should see grandpapa," I said. "Grandpapa is not well."

"You've seen it, Bawn?" my grandmother said. "I thought no one saw it but myself. But it is no use. He refuses to see a doctor. He says he will be all right in a few days."

I knew she had pulled herself up on the point of saying, "after your wedding."

Dr. Molyneux smiled humorously.

"Sure, the world's divided into two classes," he said—"the people who are always wanting to see the doctor, and the people who won't see him at all. Supposing I were to pay my respects to Lord St. Leger—it would be hardly polite to go away without doing it."

"You might be able to judge, perhaps—" began my grandmother.

"Or I might be able to get over his prejudices, Lady St. Leger. He isn't the first that wouldn't see me; and some of them couldn't see enough of me at the end," he said, getting up with that cheery confidence in his face and manner that must have put many a sick man on the road to recovery.

When my grandfather came into the drawing-room before dinner he came and kissed me, and said, "Poor little Bawn!" with an almost excessive tenderness. Afterwards he mentioned that Dr. Molyneux had said that they were not to be anxious about me.

"I didn't think one of the tribe could be so pleasant," he went on. "He is greatly interested in my swords, and knows as much of the history of weapons as I do and more, for he told me where some of them came from about which I was uncertain."

My grandmother told me afterwards with awe that Dr. Molyneux had talked about everything but health, and had had all grandpapa's collection of weapons down from the walls and out of their cases, and had not seemed to look at grandpapa except in the most casual way; but afterwards had startled her by asking, "What's on his mind, Lady St. Leger, when he isn't talking of the swords? Till that is removed I can do little for his body." I saw it was a ray of light to her through the troubles that my grandfather had taken kindly to the doctor, and I was very glad.

The next day was the last but one before my wedding, and at last the Cottage was ready for occupation. So great was my lover's desire to inhabit it that he had already moved his belongings over there from Damerstown and was sleeping there. On the afternoon of that day he came for me to go with him to see and approve of what he had done.

He was so greatly excited about it that he did not notice my reluctance to go, or perhaps he was used to my way with him, which was surely the most grudging that ever lover had to endure.

I rather thought my grandmother might have forbidden it. She had always been so particular about what a girl might not do and had not moved at all with the times in that respect. But of course everything had been altered since Richard Dawson's coming; and she only said to him not to keep me out too late as I was not over-strong.

I had thought we were going to walk, but when we had gone a little way down the avenue I saw drawn up to one side a very smart motor-brougham with a smart chauffeur on the box, and I wondered whose it might be.

"It is for you, darling," my lover replied. "Do you not like it, Bawn? It is a surprise for you."

I wished I could have thanked him better; but nothing gave me any pleasure. He put me in and tucked me up in a warm rug. It was, indeed, a most luxurious carriage, and it went like the wind.

"You give me too much," I said for the thousandth time.

"And you give me too little," he answered. "I suppose you think that is how to keep me. But I should love you just as much—I could not love you more—if you would be warmer to me."

As we went along at a speed which made the familiar roads oddly strange, all the landmarks being slurred by the speed, I looked from one side of the road to the other.

My mind was full of Anthony Cardew's messenger, the one he was so sure would break the web of lies in pieces. I said to myself that of course he could not come in time and that if he could come it would be useless. Even Anthony himself could have done nothing, since the secret was not one that we could bring into the open. Still, the air seemed full of expectation. We met very few vehicles, very few foot passengers, but at those we did meet I looked eagerly. He had been very sure that his messenger would arrive in time. And while I thrilled to that sense of expectation I felt guilty towards the man at my side, who was so generous a lover. Even now his nearness to me in the carriage that was his gift filled me with repulsion and a forlorn, shameful sense, as though I had been the wife of one man and had been given to another.

The Cottage and its grounds were enclosed within a high wall. There was a little gravel sweep running round in front of the hall door; but we left the carriage outside the green gates. Within, it was the completest thing, and I had delighted in it when old Miss Verschoyle had lived there with a companion and a cat, a dog, and a cageful of canaries. The Cottage was covered by a trellis. There were half a dozen steps to the hall door, and a window at each side. At one side of the little enclosure there was a trellis concealing, as I knew, a range of out-offices. At the other side was a stable and coach-house.

It was growing dusk now, but the Cottage was lit up. Through the unshuttered windows I could see the light of a fire and the glow of a pink-shaded lamp in the room that used to be the drawing-room. The opposite room was also fire-lit and lamp-lit.

The hall door stood wide open, and Sheila, my lover's spaniel, stood wagging her tail in the doorway.

"Your cook is already installed, darling," my lover said in the low voice which I feared in him "I told her to make herself scarce. It was not likely we should want her at such a time."

He took me in his arms and lifted me across the threshold. The little house glowed warmly, and seemed to invite us to a home. How holy, how beautiful, it would have been if the man by my side had been Anthony Cardew instead of Richard Dawson! He still held me in his arms when he had set me down and pressed me to him. I trembled with repulsion and he felt that I trembled, without understanding. He let me go almost roughly.

"Did I frighten you?" he asked, roughly tender. "You shivered, sweetheart. Oh, to think that in three days more we shall come home here never to be parted anymore!"

He was eager as a boy. In the little drawing-room a tea-table was set and a silver kettle sang above a spirit-lamp. Everything was ready for tea. There were little silver-covered dishes with spirit-lamps burning under them, and even at such a moment I could not help noticing the beauty of the Worcester cups and saucers, with pansies and tulips and roses and forget-me-nots in tiny bunches on the white.

"Let us see the rest of the house while the kettle is boiling," he said, and caught at my hand to make me go with him. But I dreaded it, this visiting which ought to have been so tender and holy. I said that I wanted some tea, that I was cold.

He put me in a deep chair and kneeling before me he chafed my hands, now and again stopping to kiss them. I was grateful when the kettle suddenly hissed and he stood up and said that for this once he was going to make the tea. So many days and years I should make it for him, sitting opposite to him and making the place where we were together Heaven by my face.

When it was ready he poured it out and brought it to me. He fed me with little pieces of hot teacake and other dainties. I took as long in drinking the tea as possible, but it could not last forever, and finally he took the cup from me, put it down, and kneeling before me again he put his arms about me.

Something in my being there alone with him, in his growing excitement, suddenly frightened me out of my wits. With a cry I pushed him away from me with both hands.

"Oh, don't!" I said; "don't you see I can't bear it? I hate it. Let me go, please." And I struggled to be free of him.

He looked up at me with a dazed expression.

"But you are going to marry me in three days," he said. "I shall be your husband. What was it you said? That you hated my caresses? You don't mean it, Bawn?"

"I do mean it," I cried, with a frantic repulsion. "I wish you had not brought me here. Please get up and let me go. I tell you I am frightened of you."

He got up and stood a little bit away from me, looking at me in a shocked bewilderment.

"But you are going to marry me?" he said. "And this is to be our home together. And you accepted me of your own free will. Do girls in love behave like this to their lovers?"

"You should not have frightened me," I cried, bursting into tears. "You should not have brought me here. How can you say I accepted you of your own free will when it is killing me? You know that I accepted you because your father holds a disgraceful secret and has frightened the life out of my grandfather and grandmother. I had to do it for them because they were old and it would kill them if the disgrace were published."

It had never entered into my mind that he could be in ignorance of how his father had constrained us, but now it flashed on my amazed mind that he had not known at all.

"Good God!" he said. "Good God!" and stood staring at me with a grey face.

I was frightened then of the mischief I had done, and sorry for him too.

"I thought you knew," I stammered.

CHAPTER XXXIII
THE END OF IT

I saw in the momentary pause that his dog came up beside him and licked his hand and he did not seem to notice her.

"You thought I knew," he repeated, his colour becoming a dull purple. "You thought I knew. And I thought your shrinking from me was but maiden modesty, and that if you did not love me you were going to love me. Why, when you trembled in my arms as I lifted you through the door I thought it was love; and all the time it was horror and repulsion. What a fool I have been! But, by Heaven—I have been fooled too!"

His expression became so wild and furious that I shrank back in my chair and covered my face with my hands.

"You needn't be afraid of me," he said; "that is all over. Come: there is nothing more to see. You had better go home."

He had regained control over himself, although his features still worked and his eyes were bloodshot. Indeed, he had such a look of suffering that I should have been sorry for him no matter how much I hated him, and now, curiously enough, my hatred seemed to have passed away.

"What are you going to do?" I asked.

"Send you home," he replied.

"But you are coming with me?"

"No. I shall not trouble Aghadoe any more by my presence. You will be quite safe with the Chauffeur."

"But what are you going to do?"

"I am not going to cut my throat, if that's what you are afraid of. I am going to—console myself as soon as I can."

I did not dare ask him how. He held his arm to me ceremoniously, and I could not help thinking that he could play the fine gentleman after all. My thoughts were so bewildered that I could not take in yet all that this involved, but seeing that he held his arm to me I took it and went out with him.

The night had come on dark outside. Looking back from the gate, I thought that the little house glowed like a ruby in the darkness.

He put me into the carriage with a careful politeness. As he wrapped the rug about me I had a sudden sense of the finality of it and the trouble that lay before me and the others, and a pity for his disappointment as well that was so poignant as to be almost unbearable.

"Forgive me," I whispered in the darkness. "I would have loved you if I could."

"Was there someone else, Bawn?" he whispered back.

"Yes, there was someone else." I felt he had a right to that truth.

"You ought to have told me," he said. "And you should not have believed that I would win you by blackmail, even though I am Garret Dawson's son."

"I am sorry. Indeed I am sorry."

I clutched at his sleeve as he was stepping out of the carriage.

"What are you going to do?" I asked again.

"Find consolation where I can. There are some ready to offer it, Bawn."

He closed the door, and I heard him telling the chauffeur to drive me to Aghadoe. I put my head out to see the last of him as we drove away, and he was standing in the darkness still looking after me.

My thoughts were in a whirl of confusion. At first I could think of nothing except that Richard Dawson himself had set me free and that his manner showed it was irrevocable. But I could not look beyond that to my Anthony's return, because how was I to tell the old people who looked to me for deliverance that I had failed them? I knew something of Garret Dawson, and that he had never in all his life been known to show mercy. His old granite face with the tight mouth and beetling eyebrows was enough. I quailed in the darkness as a vision of his face rose before me. I had no doubt that, as soon as he knew I was not going to marry his son, he would do his worst. He had been known, people said, to sacrifice business advantages even to obtain revenge.

At the thought of that I stretched out my arms as though I would take the two helpless old heads to my bosom to shelter them from the storm. How was I going to tell them? The carriage went like the wind, and I could hear the clashing of the boughs under which we passed. The stillness of the afternoon had been but the prelude to a storm.

Also the memory of Richard Dawson's face remained with me like a sore. Now that I was free of him and need dread him no more, I remembered that he had been generous and patient, and I was grieved for him. And I was troubled about that consolation which he was on the way to seek. But my own troubles were so imminent and pressing as almost to push that out. How was I going to tell them—at the last hour, too—with my wedding-dress home, and the wedding-breakfast cooking in the big kitchens, with a stir of life we had not had in Aghadoe for many a day?

It was well the journey did not take very long, or I don't know how I should have endured the strain on my nerves.

While my mind was still in confusion the carriage drew up at the front door of the Abbey. I alighted and went up the steps. The hall door stood open, and as I entered Neil Doherty came from the back. I thought he looked pale.

"Miss Bawn," he began; but I could not wait to hear him. I ran up the stairs to the drawing-room. There was no one there. I went back to the library. As I went in my grandmother came to meet me.

"I thought I heard a carriage," she said in a trembling voice. "Did Richard bring you home? What is the matter, Bawn?"

"The matter!" I repeated, "the matter! Why, the matter is that Richard Dawson will have none of me. He knew nothing of his father's bargain. When he found that I had been bought and sold for that he would have none of me. I would have gone through with it, Gran. You must forgive me and ask grandpapa to forgive me."

She stared at me with a pale face. In the pause there was a sound like a heavy sigh; then the falling of a body.

"Bawn, Bawn, what have you done?" she cried, hurrying away from me to the recess by the fireplace. "It is your grandfather. He has fainted once before this afternoon, and the doctor says it is his heart. Oh, my dear, my Toby, you have had too much to bear and it has killed you!"

She was kneeling by my grandfather and had taken his head into her lap. He had struck the fender as he fell, and the blood was flowing from a wound on his head, staining his silver hair.

Neil Doherty came rushing in. He must have been at the door to have heard the fall. He took my grandfather in his arms like a baby—it struck me sharply that he must have grown thin and light for Neil to lift him so easily—and put him on the couch.

"Whisht, your Ladyship, whisht!" he said to my grandmother. "Fetch me a drop o' water and a sponge, Miss Bawn. The cut's not a deep one. There's nothin' wrong with his Lordship, and we needn't frighten the life out o' him, wirrasthruin', when he comes back to himself. Don't tell any of the women, Miss Bawn."

I got him the water as quickly and quietly as I could, and Neil washed the blood away. The cut proved, indeed, not to be serious; but it seemed an age before my grandfather's eyes opened and he looked from Neil's face to my grandmother's.

"Have I been ill?" he asked.

"Just a bit of a wakeness, your Lordship," Neil said. "But sure, you're finely now."

I did not dare come near, but waited out of sight, dreading the time when my grandfather should remember. Presently I heard him ask for me.

"Is Bawn there?" he asked. "Where are you, child?"

I came forward and Neil withdrew. I heard the library door close behind him.

"Poor little Bawn!" my grandfather said tenderly, "poor little Bawn! We must bear whatever there is to come together, we three. God would not have this child sacrificed. I see now what a coward I was."

"Never a coward, Toby, never a coward," my grandmother cried out piteously, kissing his hand.

My grandfather put out his arm and drew me close to him.

"We must bear it together, we three," he said.

CHAPTER XXXIV

THE KNOCKING AT THE DOOR

We had dinner in the little black-panelled room off the hall, Neil waiting on us with a great assiduity. Now that the worst had happened and my grandfather's pride and courage had risen to meet it, it seemed to me that he looked better than he had looked for many months. To be sure he was very pale, but he had a look of resolution which became him, instead of the cowed and burdened look he had worn of late.

I remember that there were pheasants on the table and my grandfather asked where they had come from. There had been a constant shower of delicacies rained on us from Damerstown, and we should have grown sybarites if we had cared about such things. Neil, as though he understood, answered him that they had been shot in our own woods, and added that the fine peaches and grapes which were in a dish on the table were from our own houses. I was not sure it was true. We didn't grow peaches even in a hothouse in December; but I let it pass, and my elders were too engrossed in their thoughts to notice.

Once or twice I saw that the old couple held each other's hands below the table-cloth, and I felt that as long as they were together they could bear anything.

My grandfather ate a little of a pheasant's breast, and my grandmother followed his example; but though we made a show of eating it did not amount to very much. As for me, a curious sense of expectancy seemed to have taken possession of my mind, to the exclusion of other things. I could hardly say at what moment it had begun; but it grew till I was, in a manner of speaking, heady with it. We sat there very quiet, but all the time I was listening, not only with the ears of my body but with the ears of my heart.

After dinner Neil cleared away the dinner-things and removed the cloth. My grandmother bade him replenish the fire, and he went away and returned with a great armful of logs.

I guessed that my grandmother felt that in here we were out of sight of the preparations for the wedding which were going on everywhere else in the house.

Neil left the wine and the fruit on the table, stirred up the fire, and went away.

My grandparents sat in their chairs either side of the fireplace, I in the middle at first; but presently I changed places with my grandmother, and she sat holding Lord St. Leger's hand in hers while the firelight leaped up showing their old, careworn, troubled faces, which yet had a look of love and new peace in them.

Presently my grandfather fell asleep, and we talked in whispers, my grandmother and I. She still held his hand, and her eyes kept watching with a tender anxiety his pale face, almost as pale as a dead face, against the green velvet of the chair.

"He sleeps quietly, Bawn," she said. "He has not slept well of late."

"None of us has slept well," I said.

"It has almost broken our hearts, child, to be so cruel to you. I don't believe we have had a happy hour since it was settled. We have lain awake till cock-crow, night after night."

I had it in my mind to ask her if she had heard the ghosts, but she had never liked the talk about the ghosts, and, remembering that, I was silent.

"We ought to have faced it out," she went on. "As I said to Lord St. Leger, if the disgrace was there, there was no doing away with it, even though only Garret Dawson knew it. Mary always said she would not believe dishonour and deliberate misdoing on Luke's part. I ought to have had her faith."

"It is not too late," I said. "Let Garret Dawson publish his news! We shall see what he has to tell."

"But there is no disproving it, for Luke is dead and gone."

"On your own reasoning, dearest Gran," I said. "If we will not believe in Uncle Luke's disgrace then there is no disgrace for us. We shall only take it that Garret Dawson bears false witness. Who would believe Garret Dawson against Luke L'Estrange?"

"Ah, but you have lost your lover, my poor Bawn," she said tenderly. "You have lost Theobald, and this old house will pass away from you and him. It is all mortgaged and there is Luke's debt."

"Let it go," I said, wincing. "But as for Theobald, never fret about that, Gran. We were only brother and sister, too close to become closer."

"I think the wedding has turned Maureen's head," my grandmother went on fretfully. "I found her setting Luke's room in order. She would have it that he was coming home from school by the hooker from Galway. She has made his bed and put his room in order and she asked me at what hour she should light his fire."

"She is always madder at the full moon," I said.

"To-morrow morning we will send for Mary. She will help us to bear it. When I think of her faith I wonder that I should have had so little."

"I believe you are happier," I said wonderingly.

"I feel as though I had passed out of the hands of men into the hands of God," she replied, caressing my hair with her disengaged hand, for I had left my chair to sit down on the hearthrug by her.

Again I had that strange, acute sense of listening; but there was a storm outside, and the wind cried in the chimney and rattled the windows, and a branch of a tree tapped against the shutters—that was all.

"While your grandfather lives you will not be homeless," she said: "and who knows but that Theobald may be able to clear off the mortgages?"

My grandfather slept peacefully, as though he needed sleep; and now we talked and now we were silent, and the night wore on.

We could not move for fear of disturbing him. Dido came and lay on the rug beside me, and slept with her chin resting on my foot. I think my grandmother dozed a little and the fire went low for I was afraid to stir to replenish it. The old dog moaned and whimpered in her sleep, and my grandmother came out of her doze to say that she had been dreaming of Luke; and nodded off again.

I heard Neil Doherty bolt and bar the hall door on his way to bed and I knew then that it must be eleven. There were many things to think of. To-morrow the preparations for the wedding must all be put a stop to. The presents must be returned. There was so much to be done, so many things to be cancelled. I wondered when and how Garret Dawson's blow would fall. He was one to seek an opportunity of doing it publicly. That it would fall I had no doubt. There was no relenting behind that face of granite.

Well, for to-night the old souls might sleep. To-morrow there would be Mary Champion to stand by them. I did not yet dare to think of the joy that was coming to me from over the world. It would be another blow to them that I loved Anthony Cardew.

Also through my thoughts there came the face of Richard Dawson, and I wondered if he was somewhere out in the night. I did not feel that the house to which he was to have brought me a bride could contain him that night. What was he doing? Where had he gone for consolation? My pity for him and my remorse were great.

A coal fell out of the fire with a sudden noise, and the displaced coals fell in, sending up a big shower of sparks. The storm was at its height. It seemed to shake the solid house. And suddenly my grandmother awoke.

"Bawn, Bawn," she said, "I dreamt that your grandfather was dead and it was terrible."

At the moment my grandfather opened his eyes.

"I am very tired," he said—"very, very tired and old. If Luke is coming he ought to be here soon. Why is he not here to protect us?"

There came a sound above the crying of the wind. My grandmother had been leaning tenderly over her husband who seemed to have sunk back into his sleep; now she looked at me with a piteous terror. The wind soughed and died away, and in the pause we heard them plainly, wheels on the gravel outside that stopped at the door.

"It is the death-coach," my grandmother said. I rather saw than heard her say it, for her pale lips seemed incapable of speech.

"No, no," I cried. "It is nothing of the sort. It is the messenger I am expecting. I have been listening for him all the evening. Be quiet! He is coming for good: to help us."

But she did not seem to hear me. She had thrown both her arms about my grandfather, as though to ward off what was coming. The action awoke him, and he stood up tall and commanding as I remembered him of old, as I had not seen him for many a day.

"What is the matter, Maeve?" he asked. "You are with me. There is nothing to fear."

I noticed that the wound had opened, and his white hair was stained with blood.

"It is the death-coach," cried my grandmother.

"What matter, if it comes for both of us?" he said.

"It is not the death-coach," I cried. "It is a friend, someone come to our help. Look at Dido! She would be frightened if it were the death-coach. See how she listens!"

Above the crying of the storm there came a tremendous rat-tat on the knocker of the hall door.

CHAPTER XXXV

THE MESSENGER

My grandfather made a step or two towards the door, but my grandmother, who seemed distraught with terror, would not let him go, but clung to him the closer. Dido had gone to the door of the room and was barking to get out. She was running up and down in a frenzy of impatience. The tremendous knocking still went on above the noise of the wind.

"It is absurd," I cried, trying to make my grandmother hear; "did any one ever know the death-coach to come knocking at the door?"

But she was too terrified to hear me. So I let her be, and, snatching one of the candles from the table, I went out into the hall. I knew quite well that I should not be able to draw back the heavy bolts, but, while I looked at them helplessly, half-deafened by the incessant knocking of the great iron knocker on the oak door, old Neil came down the stairs muttering, as was his way.

"First I thought it was a ghost," he said, "but no ghost ever knocked like that. God send he brings good news, whoever he is! Glory be to God, he's in a divil of a hurry to get in."

I held my candle for him to see, and the knocking ceased while he undid the bolts. Dido was whining and running up and down impeding him, and I heard him say that he'd kick her if it wasn't that she was already afflicted with blindness, the creature, and was Master Luke's dog. Now that the silence had come we heard the rain driven in torrents against the fanlight above the hall door.

At the moment the bolt fell I glanced behind me. My grandfather and grandmother had come out into the hall: his arm was about her with a protecting tenderness. There was a huddle of women-servants in all sorts of undress, peeping from the back hall. In front of them, pushing them back, was Maureen, her shoulders covered with a shawl upon which her grey hair fell loosely.

The door burst open as soon as the bolt fell, and there was a rush of wind and rain, and my candle went out. I saw a tall figure against the stormy sky where the moon looked through the fast-driven clouds.

"God save us, what a night!" the new-comer said, entering and closing the door behind him; and it took all his strength to close it.

"Bring lights, bring lights," I cried; and ran to my grandfather to whisper to him to take my grandmother back into the room lest the sudden joy should be too much for her. For I had seen old

Dido leap on to the stranger with a frantic joy, licking his face and hands; or I had known that it was so without seeing it, for the hall was in darkness.

Some one brought a light, and I saw old Maureen leap at the tall stranger as Dido had done and fling her arms about him, crying out for her Ladyship, where was her Ladyship, for Master Luke had come home.

And after that everything was confusion for a few minutes, and I can scarcely remember what happened in the babel of voices all crying out and rejoicing at once.

"See that the horse is put up for the night and that the man has food and shelter," I heard Uncle Luke say to Neil.

Then he, Uncle Luke, passed through the affectionate crowd that seemed as if it would eat him with joy. I saw him go to his father and mother, put an arm about each and pass within the little room, and there after a moment I followed them.

They were all three standing on the hearthrug when I came in, and Uncle Luke had one arm about his mother and the other thrown across his father's neck.

"So this is little Bawn," he said, letting them go, and coming forward to meet me. "So this is little Bawn."

I should have known his blue eyes and smile anywhere, I thought, although his hair was as if dust had been sprinkled over it, and there were deep lines in the face I remembered as being very merry. I had a passing wonder that in this moment he remembered my existence or recognized me, for Lord and Lady St. Leger were still dumb or inarticulate with joy, and could not have spoken of me.

"Yes, I am Bawn," I said, lifting my face to kiss him. "I am so glad you have come home, Uncle Luke."

"I should have come long ago," he said. "Yet, thank God, I come in time. I have messages for you, little Bawn, to be delivered later."

So he, he of all people, was Anthony's messenger!

He put his arm about me and we returned to the old couple by the fire.

"We were kept back by the storm," he said. "Oh, how I fretted and fumed lest I should arrive too late! And Mary Champion, how is she? Is she maid or wife or widow?"

"She never married, for your sake, Uncle Luke," I said, speaking up boldly. "You will see her to-morrow morning."

Then I saw that he still wore his heavy cloak, and I made him take it off; and he put his mother in one chair and his father in another and sat down between them, and I came and sat on the rug at their feet.

"We thought you were dead," his father said, looking at him with an air of beatitude.

"I never did," said the mother. "And Maureen did not. Nor did Mary Champion. Luke, Luke, why did you stay away so long?"

"Because I thought I was best dead, little mother. Because I thought I should have to stand my trial for murder if I came back. I have lived in the waste places of the world since I left you, or I must have known. I say waste places, yet they are beautiful, fruitful places of the earth; only there are few white men there and those adventurers. For beauty and kindliness it was the Garden of Eden; but there has never been a day when I was not sick for Aghadoe."

"And how did you know at last?" his father asked. His mother could only look at him with shining eyes.

"Why, someone came from these parts to enlighten my blindness. He was hunting for treasure. I knew where the treasure lay, twenty fathoms deep, in a little bay of an island in the South Seas. What use was treasure to me since I could not come home? I have known murder and worse done over treasure. I knew it was there, and I let it be. The gentle, brown people of the islands had no use for it. It would only have brought in lawless and desperate men to disturb the peace of that Garden of Eden. Now it makes me a rich man. It makes him in whose charge I have left it a rich man. He will bring home the treasure. Like me, he thinks of it only as a means to an end."

"You will be able to pay the mortgage," my grandfather said, with an air of immense relief.

Then he seemed to remember something; and he cried out suddenly that Garret Dawson held an I.O.U. which Uncle Luke had given to Sir Jasper Tuite for five thousand guineas.

"He said it would hang you," the poor old man went on, sobbing and stumbling in his speech, "because, of course, it would prove that you had a motive for shooting Jasper Tuite. He said other things, dreadful for a father and mother to hear."

"But you did not believe them!" Uncle Luke said. "You did not believe them! I did owe Jasper Tuite five thousand guineas. It was a card debt. I should have known better than to play with a man of his reputation; but I repaid it, every penny. I have his receipt for it. What else, father?"

"That there was a girl, a girl whom—I should not speak of such things in Bawn's presence and your mother's—whom you had wronged. She had been on the stage in Dublin, and she accounted for your extravagance at that time. He said that Jasper Tuite came between you, tried to save the girl from you. He said it would be a pretty case to go before a jury, that you had cause, even more than the money, to hate Jasper Tuite and wish him out of the way."

"And you believed it?"

I saw Lord St. Leger cower, and I said out of my pity and love for him—

"Uncle Luke, he is old, and you had left him He could not disprove the things even if he did not believe them."

Uncle Luke's face changed. He looked down at his father.

"We will give him the lie together," he said; and then he noticed the blood on the white hair and was terrified, till we assured him it was nothing. "So little Bawn was the price of Garret Dawson's silence," he said; and then added solemnly that he could never have forgiven himself if the price had been paid.

At this point the door of the room was opened, and Neil Doherty, bowing on the threshold, announced that supper was served. And we remembered that Uncle Luke must be hungry, and his mother reproached herself, while he remembered for the first time that he had not eaten for many hours.

I don't know how Neil had managed it in the time, but the house was lit from top to bottom and the servants were standing in a line for us to pass through, all with happy faces. And Maureen stood at the head of them, as though she only had the right.

Uncle Luke gave his arm to my grandmother and I took my grandfather's, and we went up in state, with old Dido following us, to the dining-room, where supper was spread and all the silver plate was set out. There was a roaring fire in the grate and every candle in the big chandelier had been lit, and all was as though the coming of the heir had been long foreseen.

I do not think that in any house in the kingdom there was that night such joy and thanksgiving as in Aghadoe Abbey.

CHAPTER XXXVI

THE OLD LOVERS

After a little while I went away and left them together.

Uncle Luke came with me to the dining-room door and lit my candle for me as though he had never gone away. When he had lit it he went with me outside the door, and, partly closing it, he said to me—

"Tell me, Bawn dear, did Mary Champion believe those lies?"

"She knew nothing of them," I answered. "They would not tell her the things Garret Dawson had said. But she would not have believed them. She was vexed with them for being afraid, because she said she never would believe that you had done anything which could bring disgrace on any one who loved you."

"My brave girl!" he said softly; and then he said to me with a smile that I had the handsomest and noblest gentleman in the world for a lover, and that my Anthony was coming to me as fast as he could and that they two were sworn brothers.

I ought to have slept the soundest and sweetest sleep in the world, especially as the storm had died down and the ghosts cried no longer and there seemed an atmosphere of peace and happiness over all the house. But I was disturbed in my dreams by the face of Richard Dawson, who had loved me so much to his own hurt and in my dream I was weeping.

The household was barely astir when I awoke next morning and there was a frosty air. I lay watching the window awhile as the dark gave place to dusk. It would be an hour yet before the sun should rise; and a maid came to light my fire and bring me my tea and my bath-water. But I was too excited to sleep, so I got up and dressed myself in the half light, and when I was ready I put on my outdoor things and went down the stairs. I met only a young maid sweeping the stairs with her brush and dustpan, and she looked at me as though she thought the joy had driven me mad.

"I shall be back to breakfast, Katty," I said. "It is a beautiful frosty morning for a walk."

"You're not going to walk in the dark, Miss Bawn?" she said, and stood staring after me over the banisters when I answered her that the sun would soon be up.

I liked the frosty keenness of the air, and this morning my heart was very light. Although it had rained so heavily in the night the frost had turned everything hard and stiff; but as I ran on my way down the long avenue, and heard the sleepy twittering of the birds, I could have sung for the new, healthy life that was in my veins. I had not gone far before the sun sent his golden rays above the horizon, and the blue came out in the sky overhead and it was day, and all at once the robins began to sing.

The early walk gave me a pleasant sense of adventure. I was on my way to Castle Clody, and was wondering if I should find my godmother up and how I would tell her the good news.

By the time I arrived there the whole lawn and the hedges were shining with the diamonds of the frost in the good golden light, and glancing up at my godmother's window I saw that her blind was up, and said to myself that she must be awake and about. Of course she was always an early riser, though she would have me lie late a-bed when I stayed with her, saying it was good for young people to sleep.

The doors and windows of Castle Clody were always open to the fresh air; and as I went in by the open hall door I saw my godmother coming down the stairs.

"Why, bless me, it is Bawn!" she said. "What brings you so early, child? There is no bad news, I trust. Your grandmother?"

"Was never better in her life. Godmother dear, so many things have happened that I do not know where to begin."

"Begin somewhere," she said, after one quick look at me, and led the way into the little room where we usually had our meals together. The fire was lit and the table set for breakfast, and the room looked very pleasant. "Dido is not with you," she said, closing the door behind us.

"No," I returned.

"And how is that, Bawn? How did she let you come alone?"

"As I came down the stairs in the dusk of the morning she lay on the mat outside Uncle Luke's door, and when I called to her to come she wagged her old tail and would not come. For the first time she would not follow me. Godmother dear, isn't it a strange thing that Maureen should have prepared his room yesterday, saying that he would be with us before night?"

"Bawn, Bawn," cried my godmother, very pale, "if you do not mean that Luke L'Estrange has come home I can never forgive you."

"And I should deserve not to be forgiven," I said. "He has come home."

"I knew he was not dead."

"He is alive and well, and one of the first inquiries he made was for you."

"Now they shall see," she said exultantly, and her lips curled, "how much truth there was in those slanders of Garret Dawson's. Dear old souls! why were they afraid? Why would they not let me challenge him?"

"They were not so foolish," I said. "He held papers. If Uncle Luke had not come home we could not have disproved them."

"And there is an end to your marriage?" she asked breathlessly.

I held out my hand to her. It no longer carried Richard Dawson's ring.

"He set me free last night," I said, "before we knew who was coming home. You must clear him in your thoughts, godmother. He never knew how his father had obtained our consent to the marriage. He was furious when he knew and he set me free. I wish I knew what had become of him."

"Don't trouble about him, child. Presently you will find a lover worthy of you."

I said nothing, but my heart leaped. I was a proud woman to think that Anthony Cardew loved me, and still I was grieved for the others.

"You will breakfast with me, child?" she went on.

"I am furiously hungry," I replied. "And afterwards—will you come back with me to Aghadoe?"

"I think not. If your uncle wants me he will find me here."

"I think he will see Garret Dawson first. He will not come to you till all that is cleared up."

"It need never be cleared for me. Whatever the story was, it is for me as though it never existed."

I made a most prodigious breakfast. I had no anxiety as to what they might think about my absence at Aghadoe; I felt they would know where I was.

I said no more to my godmother about returning with me. I felt she was right in waiting for Uncle Luke where she was, and I was sure he would go to her when he had confronted Garret Dawson and wrung the truth from him. But after breakfast, lest they should be waiting for me at Aghadoe, I returned home the way I had come, feeling as though I walked on air. I could have run and leaped, except when a thought came to me of Richard Dawson, and then my heart was suddenly heavy.

I entered the woods by the postern gate, and hurried along with a heart full of gratitude to the kind God who had brought good out of evil and had delivered us from our troubles.

Just at the edge of the wood someone stepped from one of the side paths full in my way. It was Richard Dawson, and I was amazed at the havoc the sufferings of one night had wrought in him.

"Don't be afraid of me, Bawn," he said. "I'm not here to trouble you, only there is something I want to give you. Here are those precious papers my father held. I have been waiting here for some chance messenger to take them. They are my gift to you. Let Lord St. Leger see that he has everything and then destroy them."

He held out a sealed packet to me and I took it.

"Everything is there," he said. "Henceforth we are as harmless as a snake that has had its poison-bag out. Think kindly of me, Bawn. I am going a long journey. I have had a scene with my father. He swears that not a penny of his money shall come to me. What matter? I shall do without it very well. Good-bye, Bawn."

"God-speed," I said, altering the word of farewell.

He turned round and came back to me.

"Nay, not God-speed," he said harshly. "God has little to do with such as I am."

And then he was gone.

CHAPTER XXXVII

THE JUDGMENT OF GOD

I walked into the dining-room and found Uncle Luke at breakfast, with Lord and Lady St. Leger on each side of him, eating little themselves, but pressing one thing after another on him.

I felt a sense of a new alertness about the house. Although the old servants were faithful they had grown a little slipshod in their ways, seeing that it mattered little to their employers. Now things had suddenly assumed a swept and garnished air. One felt that the master had come home.

They all looked up at me with some expectation when I came in.

"Where have you been so early, Bawn?" my grandmother asked, while Uncle Luke came and set a chair for me and stood smiling at me; I was glad that in those waste places of the earth he had not forgotten those fine debonair ways which of old had made the women fall in love with him.

"I have been to Castle Clody," I answered.

"I thought as much. Why did not Mary come back with you? Was she transported at the good news?"

"She thought perhaps that Uncle Luke would—"

I paused for words. I had a feeling that even in this case, where I was sure that Uncle Luke cared for his old love, I should respect my godmother's dignity. Even Luke L'Estrange ought not to be sure that she expected him.

"I thought she would have come to rejoice with us," my grandmother said disappointedly; and my grandfather's face showed that he, too, did not understand the constant friend's absence in the hour of great joy.

"Is it that she cannot forgive us?" he muttered.

But the lover knew better than that.

"To be sure I must go to her," he said. "It would not be fitting that she should come to me. I would have been earlier astir than Bawn; I would have been waiting for her doors to open, only that, there is something that must be done first."

"I don't think there is anything you need wait for, Uncle Luke," I said, handing the sealed packet to my grandfather. "I met Richard Dawson on my way back. He was waiting for someone to carry his message. He told me that my grandfather was to examine these papers, to see that everything was there, and afterwards to burn them."

My grandfather seized the papers eagerly. His hand shook so that he could not open them, and he fumbled for his glasses.

"You have a son now, sir," said Uncle Luke, putting an arm about his shoulder.

They went away to the window to examine the papers, and for some time there was silence in the room. At last my uncle gathered the lot together and going to the fire placed them on top of it. They caught; and in a few seconds there was no trace of them.

"How little or how much of this Garret Dawson believed to be true I leave to his Maker," he said, turning about as the last ash went up the chimney. "For his son's sake I shall not try to punish him. I believe some of these letters were forged. I will show you one of these days letters from the girl I saved from Jasper Tuite. For that is how it was. She is an honoured wife and mother of children. It is one of the few things in my life of which I may be proud."

Afterwards he went away and we knew that he was gone to Castle Clody.

There was so much to be done and I had to do it all; Lord and Lady St. Leger could only be silent together, gazing into each other's eyes, praising God humbly for their son given back from the dead. I left them in the sunshine on the terrace creeping up and down, and as I looked back before I entered the house by the French windows of the morning-room, I recognized all at once that my grandmother had put off her black, and was wearing grey, with some of her old lace trimming it. It was a tabinet which I must have seen in my childhood. The memory of it was so remote that I felt as if I must have read about it; but I had an exact memory of the way it was made, which was billowing about the feet, and with a very straight bodice. While I looked at them she picked a rose from the wall and fastened it into her husband's coat.

I was busy till lunch-time, putting up packets and addressing them. When at last I went downstairs I found Uncle Luke and my godmother in the drawing-room. The years seemed to have slipped away from her. Her dear brown face was as shy and rapturous as the face of any young girl in love who knows she is beloved. They were standing by the fire when I went in.

My godmother had one foot on the fender and her hand supported her cheek. As I went up to her, I saw in the mirror that she was wearing a very beautiful ring of sapphires which I had noticed on Uncle Luke's hand.

She kissed me almost timidly, with her eyes down.

"She has taken me back again, Bawn," said Uncle Luke.

"He would not listen to me when I said I was too old," said my dear godmother.

In the dining-room Neil Doherty was bustling about with an air of great importance. Lord and Lady St. Leger had not yet come in.

"Sure, it never rains but it pours," Neil said, lifting a bottle of wine from the hearth where he had put it to take the chill off. "There's a great stir in the country. 'Tisn't enough to have Master Luke walking in to us safe and sound last night, but Garret Dawson's been found dead in his study. They didn't dare disturb him when he was busy. At last when Mrs. Dawson herself sent he was dead. A good riddance to bad rubbish, say I."

It was no use rebuking Neil for his want of charity to the dead. I knew there were worse things being said of Garret Dawson by every peasant. We were silent, awed, by this sudden and awful happening. I thought of poor comfortable Mrs. Dawson, and felt that, tyrant as he had been to her, she would grieve for him as though he had been a pattern of all the virtues. Yet she had her son. A thought came to me that Garret Dawson had not had time to disinherit his son after all.

"Poor Master Richard!" Neil went on, averting his eyes on me. "'Tis all over the country that last night Tom Jordan of Clonmany escaped from his bed in the small-pox hospital. About three o'clock this morning Master Richard Dawson brought him back in that quare carriage of his that brought you home last night, Miss Bawn. Tom's mortal bad this mornin'. 'Tis pretty sure Master Richard'll get the disease for he lifted Tom in his arms. I wonder what for at all was he driving round the country that hour of the night?"

"No matter what he was driving for, he was there to good purpose," said my godmother.

"True for you, Miss Mary," Neil responded placidly.

And I, too, I wondered how it was that Richard Dawson had been abroad at such an hour of the night. But I did not wait to think of that. I was proud and glad of the thing he had done, and I remembered how I had said to him that he was brave and how pleased he had been.

CHAPTER XXXVIII

CONFESSION

Christmas passed and the dark days turned round to New Year, and New Year came and there were great clumps of snowdrops pushing up their delicate, drooping heads in all the shrubberies, neighbouring the patches of snow, for we had had a white Christmas and a white New Year.

We had settled down to the new ways of life as though the old had not been. There was perfect peace and happiness at Aghadoe. In the spring the workmen were to set to work at the task of renovating the Abbey. Uncle Luke and my godmother were to be married before Lent, quietly. As for me, I waited, till my whole life had become one expectation.

After the funeral at Damerstown was over I had gone to see Mrs. Dawson, having ascertained first that her son was absent for a few days. The poor woman had wept over me and forgiven me.

"Rick told me all," she said. "Sure, I wish you could have cared for him for himself. Only his mother knows how much good there is in him. And, dear, you must try to forgive him that's gone."

"We have forgiven him," I said, "as we hope for forgiveness."

Then she wept again softly, and poured out to me her hopes and fears for her boy.

"It's gone deep with him, dear," she said: "it's gone very deep with him. But, sure, we must trust to God to bring good out of the trouble. He'd never have done you that wrong to marry you and you fond of someone else. You don't mind my knowing, dear? My boy tells me everything. Sure, I'd have known it, for if there was no one else you must have cared for Rick."

"Someone else will care for him," I said.

"Indeed, I wouldn't mind who he married if she was good and fond of him and would keep him at home. He won't leave me now, not for a bit—till I'm happier; but he says it's best he should go, that he has a reason for going. Ah, well; he'll settle down some time, when he's got over this."

It might have been three weeks later when we heard that Richard Dawson had taken the small-pox and was lying ill at the Cottage. The illness was complicated, it was feared, by his having driven in the night to the small-pox hospital and asked to be taken in there, but there had been a recrudescence of the plague, and the place was crowded to the doors. Dr. Molyneux was working there like ten men, and it was his idea to have Richard Dawson taken to the Cottage, which was much nearer than Damerstown. We heard that the night journey, which was like to cost him his life, had been undertaken when he found the illness coming on, to prevent as much as might be the danger of infection to the large household at Damerstown. He was very ill indeed, and the doctors hardly thought he could live.

I was so sorry for him that I felt that if he died even the happiness of my meeting with my lover would be clouded over. I longed for news of him, but it was not very easy to obtain it, since the infection kept every one away.

But one day I was walking when I met Lady Ardaragh driving in her little phaeton. I had not seen her for some time and I was amazed at the change in her appearance. She looked terribly ill. All her butterfly prettiness was gone, and there was something to make the heart ache to see such evident suffering in one who had had the round softness of a child.

She pulled up her ponies as soon as she saw me.

"Bawn, Bawn," she said, "there is nothing but trouble in the world—at least in my world. Stay where you are, child; don't come too near me. Do you know that he is dying over there?"

She pointed with her whip in the direction of the Cottage.

"I think I am mad to-day, Bawn," she went on: "and if I do not speak to someone I shall surely go mad. I wish I were a Roman Catholic and could confess to a priest. How much wiser they are than those who deny the necessity of confession! I have always been fond of you, Bawn. I believe you are as true as steel. Let me confess to you and save my reason."

"No, no," I said; "you are not yourself to-day. You will be sorry afterwards. There is Sir Arthur."

"If you will not listen to me I shall go to him, and there will be an end to everything. Perhaps I am mad. It's enough to drive any woman mad. Richard Dawson is dying; and my little Robin is sickening. They will not let me be with him till they know if it is the small-pox. Isn't it enough to drive a woman mad?"

"Tell me, you poor soul," I said—"tell me everything. Afterwards it will be buried at the bottom of the sea."

She turned to me with a sick look of gratitude.

"You don't know how it will ease me," she said. "I had a thought of going to Quinn by the light railway and going into the Catholic Chapel there and finding a priest who would listen to me and absolve me. But I was afraid I should be seen and recognized. When they told me Robin was sickening I knew it was a judgment of God."

"God doesn't judge in that way," I said. "Perhaps it is in that way He calls you back. I have no belief in an angry God!"

"You have not, Bawn? I was brought up on it. It turned me away from religion. You think God will not take the child away from me because of my sin?"

The anguished soul in her eyes implored me. God forgive me if it was presumptuous, but I said—

"I am so sure of His mercy that I am sure He will not."

"If He will spare me Robin, I will be a good woman for the future. Arthur has been very tender to me over the child. It was he who banished me from Robin's room, although he is there himself. He says that I am so precious to him that the world would fall in ruins without me. Why didn't he say it to me before, and not live always in a world which I could not enter? Bawn, I have never really loved any one but my husband."

"I am sure of it," I said, "as he never loved anyone but you."

"Oh, the folly of it all!" she moaned, sitting huddled up in her little phaeton, with her eyes looking miserably before her.

Then she turned her gaze on me, and I felt as though her unhappy eyes scorched and burned me.

"Yet I very nearly ran away with Richard Dawson," she said. "In fact, I did run away with him that night after you had broken with him. He concealed nothing from me. He did not even pretend to love me. And I went with him on those terms. As the mercy of God would have it, we found that poor wretch in the road not twenty yards from my own gates. It seemed to sober us. We were both mad. He would not let me touch him. He told me to go back; that it was all over. I crept back. By the mercy of God I had left a door ajar. I crept back to my room, and none knows that I ever left it except he and I and you. Bawn, am I not mad to tell you such a story? You, an innocent girl! I must be mad to tell my shame to any one when it might die with him and be buried with me."

"The mercy of God met you at every step and saved you," I said, feeling how little equal I was to the task of comforting her.

"Of course you despise me," she said: and the hard misery was gone out of her eyes and voice; "but I have confessed. You will never look at me again, but you have taken the weight off my life that was crushing it."

I could only answer her in one way. I crossed the distance she had set between us, and took her in my arms and kissed her.

"I shall be your loving friend forever," I said, while she pushed me away and cried out that I must not touch her, lest she should have the infection about her.

"Although I never touched him, Bawn, I never touched him," she kept on assuring me. "He would not permit it. Bawn, if he is to die, don't you think God will forgive him his sins because of that great act of charity? The poor creature was horrible, horrible. I ran away from him when the lamps were turned on his face. But Richard Dawson was not afraid."

"It was splendid of him," I said. "I am sure God has forgiven him."

"And I need not tell my husband? I have felt ever since that I must confess to him. If I did he might forgive me, but it would never be the same again. Now I have slaked my thirst for confession by telling you. Bawn, do you think I must tell him?"

I felt as though I answered her with a voice and an authority not my own.

"You must never tell him," I said. "You owe it to him not to destroy his happiness. If you have ever the need for confession again, come to me."

"I will, Bawn dear, and God bless you," she said, her face lighting. "You have helped me so much. Perhaps, after all, Robin may not be sickening for the small-pox. What a thing that would be!"

"If he is he will still be in the hands of God," I said.

For many days after that I waited for news of Richard Dawson so eagerly that it seemed to break in upon my expectation.

One thing I knew at least, and that was that love was nursing him. The information came to me through Maureen, in a characteristic manner. Even the happiness of these days did not make Maureen gentle.

"You've heard about Nora Brady, Miss Bawn?" she said.

"No?"

My heart sank, apprehending some new calamity; while Maureen went on in bitter tones—

"I never thought well of her and now I'm proved right. The minute she heard that Master Richard was took with the small-pox she ran off to him like a mad thing. And there she is ever since. Not a womankind in the house but herself. Her mother was a decent woman; I'm glad she didn't live to see it."

"And if she did, Maureen," I said sternly, "she might be proud of her girl. It isn't possible that you are making scandal out of Nora's mercy to the sick? I think it most noble, most Christian of her. I honour her for it."

"Whisht, child!" said Maureen, scornfully. I shall never inspire respect in Maureen's breast. "I know what I know. To be sure, you'd be the last to know of it, of the walks and the talks with Master Richard. Everyone knew except yourself."

"Be silent, Maureen," I said, asserting myself for once. "I know everything, everything. And I know that Nora is a good, innocent girl. Don't dare to speak to others as you have spoken to me."

And then I was contrite, seeing my old nurse quail before me, for I had never shown her that I could be angry.

CHAPTER XXXIX

THE BRIDEGROOM COMES

About the last week of February my joy came home. I remember that it was exquisite weather, the blackbird singing his passionate song in the bare boughs fit to break your heart with its beauty. There were high, white, shining clouds on the blue, and the mountains were grey-lavender. The wall-flower clumps were in bloom in the courtyard of the Abbey, and there were many primroses and delicate primulas in the garden; and all the hyacinths were out withindoors, making a delicious smell.

I went to meet my joy with a heart in which there was no sorrow. Richard Dawson was out of danger, and little Robin Ardaragh's case had proved to be merely chicken-pox. I met them out driving, and Robin was on his mother's knee, and his father was looking at the pair as though the world contained nothing else. They pulled up when they saw me; and Lady Ardaragh cried out to me—

"Bawn, Bawn, I am the happiest woman alive."

"And I the happiest man," said Sir Arthur, seriously. "Would you believe it, Miss Devereux, that she thought I cared more for my books than for her? As though anything could give me consolation without her!"

Then Lady Ardaragh cried out that they were a pair of egotists and pulled me down to kiss her, saying that she wished me joy, for everyone knew by this time that Anthony Cardew was my lover and was coming home to me.

We were very quiet at the Abbey. A fortnight earlier Uncle Luke and my godmother had been married, and were now spending a quiet honeymoon at Killarney. They were going to live at Castle Clody when they returned; and there was a great ado making preparations for them, and every day I was over there, sometimes with my grandmother, to see that things were going on as they should.

By this time, long before this indeed, my grandparents knew all about Anthony, and were reconciled to the idea of my marrying a Cardew. Indeed, there had never been anything against my Anthony, for he was one of those whom everybody loved and admired. But the shadowy barrier was down, and they had rejoiced that I was to marry the man who had been instrumental in bringing Luke home after all those years. My grandmother said even that she was glad there had been no attachment of the sort between me and Theobald, since she had no liking for a marriage of first cousins.

By this time also we had Miss Travers' portrait, and she and Theobald were engaged. She was a very sweet-looking girl, and so much prettier than I, having delicate little features and beautiful brown eyes and red lips, that I was not surprised Theobald had forgotten his old fancy for me.

She was coming home in the summer and was to stay at Aghadoe, and Theobald was to follow her in the autumn and they were to be married. My grandmother was rather nervous about the prospect of receiving her alone.

"For, of course, you will be on your travels, Bawn," she said; "and although Luke and Mary will be at Castle Clody, it will not be the same thing as if they were here. But I must love her, seeing that she will be Theobald's wife, and, please God, the mother of the heir—that is, after Luke and Theobald, of course."

I was glad my godmother was not there to hear, lest it should hurt her, for she loved children and ought to have been the mother of a houseful of them.

Now that my expectation was to be fulfilled within a few days I became oddly frightened of it. Supposing he found that he did not love me after all, that he had been misled by a fancied resemblance in me to the miniature! Supposing, supposing ... I put away thoughts of calamity from me with both hands. God was too good to let anything happen to him now.

I was so fidgety and restless that I felt I worried the old couple. I could settle to nothing. I could not read, although I had always been a greedy reader. I was living my own love-story too keenly to be put off with imaginary ones. Music held me for a little while; but through it I was listening—listening for his coming, or for the telegram that should announce the arrival of his boat at Southampton. I used to look across at the lighted table by the fire where my grandparents played cribbage night after night, and wonder at the quiet old faces. Would Anthony and I come to be like that? So interested in the chance of a card, so content to sit quietly in a chimney-corner? I could not believe it of Anthony. He would be always like a sword, like a flame.

I went and came now to Brosna as one who had a right. I would come in upon Terence Murphy scrubbing a floor or polishing silver or some such thing, and he would look up as my shadow fell on him.

"Any news, Miss Bawn?"

"None, Terence, not yet."

"Ah, well; sure, it's on its way. There's nothing like being ready in time."

Day after day now he lit the fires in Anthony's rooms. Day after day I went across and gathered the little lavender primulas, the faint, garden primroses, the crocuses and violets and wall-flowers, and filled bowls and vases with them. I believe Terence Murphy used to wait up till the small hours, lest by chance his master should come unannounced. Always the house stood ready for him, like our hearts. I knew Anthony's faithful servant loved him like a dog, and it endeared him to me. Through February our waiting prolonged itself.

The 28th of February was a day of balmy airs. There was a light mist on the grass, and as you walked it was through a silver web of gossamers. Gossamers hung on every briarbush and floated about the fields. The raindrops of last night jewelled them in the rays of the sun. Dido and I broke whole silver forests on our morning walk to Brosna.

I remember that the blackbird was singing deliciously, yet less poignantly sweet than he should sing at dusk. There was a mysterious stir and flutter of spring in all the coppices. A quiet south wind marshalled the pearly clouds before it as though it were a shepherd driving a flock to the fold.

As I entered Brosna by the garden-way I noticed that Terence had run up the Irish flag on the flagstaff which he had placed on the little lawn outside Anthony's rooms, and I remembered that it was the anniversary of a battle in which my Anthony had covered himself with glory.

In the sheltered garden it was very warm. The sun drew out the aromatic odours from the hedges and borders of box. Terence had been polishing up the dial. It winked in the sun, and as I passed I stopped to read the inscription—

"I count only the golden hours."

There was no stir of Terence about. Usually one heard him singing or whistling or shouting half a mile away. I saw to my vases. I looked into the room which Anthony used as a dining-room when he was at home, and saw the table set, the old damask table-cloth, patched and darned by Terence himself, warmly white, the silver and glass shining. I smiled as I noticed that two places had been set. It was as though Terence anticipated the wonderful days to come.

Anthony's chair was drawn in front of the fire, which had been lately attended to, for the hearth was clean, and a log of cherry-wood burning on the coals sent out a delicious fragrance. Presently Terence would come bustling in to ask, "What news, Miss Bawn?" Sitting in the chair in front of the warm fire, full of beatific dreams, I somehow fell asleep.

I had been dreaming the most wonderful things, and when I started out of my sleep I thought I was still dreaming. Anthony was kneeling by me. His arms were about me.

"I've been watching you for the last half-hour," he said; "and, faith, I couldn't wait any longer for a kiss. Did I frighten you, darling? You looked so much like an angel that you half-frightened me. What have you been doing to yourself? You were round and soft the last time I held you. There is some change."

"You should have seen me two months ago," I said, "when I was going to die of marrying any man but you."

"Ah, Bawn, darling, is it only that you are taking pity on my white head? What is it that you see in me? I am twice your age, child."

"And the finest gentleman in the three kingdoms," I said, stroking his hair. "So fine a gentleman that you are out of date. The commonplace world doesn't grow fine gentlemen like you nowadays."

Afterwards we had our first meal together. They would not expect me back yet to lunch, and Anthony had arrived hungry as a hunter, while he protested that a man as much in love as he had no right to be hungry.

He had walked in unexpectedly, but Terence had not been taken by surprise. Terence had things ready as though he had known the day and hour of his coming. He served us as excellent a meal, according to my Anthony, as had ever been eaten. As for me, I did not know what it consisted of, but only that Anthony and I sat opposite to each other and that Anthony's eyes upon me made me sometimes fain to cover my own with my hands, and that when Terence Murphy went out of the room Anthony would come round the table to kiss me. He said that the meal together was a stolen joy; something he had no right to till after we were married. He said a great many happy, foolish things. As for me, it was a meal in Elysium.

CHAPTER XL

KING COPHETUA

All that is long ago, and I am Bawn Cardew, who was Bawn Devereux. We have a boy, dark and fine, like Anthony, and a girl who resembles me. I am still in a bewilderment as to why Anthony should have chosen me. I believe there is no woman, gentle or simple, who comes in contact with him, from my grandmother down to Katty McCann, the beggar-woman, who is not in love with him. His way with women is always beautiful. I have seen him carry a tramp's squalling child up a steep hill and hand it to the mother at the top with the courtesy he would show to a duchess. Elderly and plain women love him especially, because he is not aware that they are elderly and plain. And men look up to him and admire him just as much after their fashion.

As I write I am in my own little morning-room at Brosna, which love has made beautiful for me. Outside I see velvet lawns and bright flower-beds, and beyond the lawns and the ha-ha I can see in the park a herd of deer feeding. At the moment it is quiet. Then I hear the thud-thud of hoofs. Our boy comes riding by on a little rough mountain pony. Terence Murphy is giving him his riding lesson. He sits in the saddle as straight as his father, although he is little more than a baby. He will have Anthony's straight, strenuous, clean look, like a blade or a flame.

And there comes Anthony himself with little Bawn on his shoulder. Her golden hair falls about his white head. There is not a grey hair in his black moustache, nor in his fine, even, black eyebrows. They go on after the pony. Presently they will come shouting for me. They are my world; but I have room for affections outside.

Brosna is now what it was meant to be, a stately, beautiful, well-kept house. We are rich: the treasure made us all rich; and that is a strange thing enough in our country, where there is no money to spare among the gentle-folk.

And talking of wealth reminds me of Richard Dawson.

It was the week before my marriage—that was Holy Week, and I was married on the Easter Tuesday—when I received a letter from Mrs. Dawson of Damerstown, asking me to come and see her. The letter accompanied a gift so beautiful and costly that if I had liked her less I should have been inclined to return it.

As it was, I let Anthony do without me for once. To be sure, he was tremendously busy getting Brosna in order for me. I had Zoe brought round, the beautiful mare who was his latest gift to me, and rode over to Damerstown.

Mrs. Dawson received me in the drawing-room, affectionate as of old, but with the air which asked forgiveness for the wrong her husband had done us. It was an air that grieved me, and as I kissed her I passed my hand over her forehead as though I would brush it away like a palpable thing.

"I thought, dearie," she said, "being what you are, that you'd be happier in your own happiness if you knew things were well with my poor Rick. He never did you any harm except to love you too much."

"No, indeed," I said hastily, "and I should be so glad to know that he has forgiven and forgotten me. I've heard, of course, that he has quite recovered and is going abroad. I shall always feel very kindly towards him and very sorry because of any wrong I did him."

"You never did him any," the mother said.

It was on the tip of my tongue to ask her where Nora Brady was, for that was a trouble to me, too, despite my happiness. The poor people round about had, I was told, taken the same view of poor Nora's devotion to her sick man as Maureen. She had slipped away from those who, like myself, would have stood her friends. But before I could ask the question Richard Dawson himself came into the room.

I was startled and a little embarrassed at first sight of him. I had had no idea that he was at Damerstown. And his face was sadly marked and pitted with the small-pox.

"Miss Devereux, you must forgive my presenting myself before you with this hideous face, but there are some things I want to tell you. There, don't look at me! Take this."

He picked up a Japanese fan and handed it to me and the action hurt me. I compelled myself to look at him without flinching.

"You are not at all hideous," I said. "No one who cared for you would think you hideous."

"Why, no," he said. "My mother looks at me as though I had the skin of a young child—and there is another— Miss Bawn, I wish you happiness. I am very glad the better man has won."

"You are very generous."

While we talked Mrs. Dawson got up and left us. She was one of those people who are always forgetting things and going in search of them, so the action had no special significance.

"You are very generous," I said. And then I asked him the question which was in my mind. "Mr. Dawson," I said, "can you tell me where Nora is? I want to write to her, to bring her back."

"I know," he answered, "but she will not come back yet awhile. She has, by her own wish and desire, gone to school, to a convent. She had schooling enough for me, God knows, in her tender and faithful heart; but she is as obstinate as any creature ever was when she thinks a thing is right. So I have to wait, very much against my will, while the nuns make a lady of Nora. It is her own phrase. I have assured her that she is a better lady than most ladies I have known, and that I am not a gentleman. But she would banish me and try my patience."

"Meaning—?"

"Meaning—that she will marry me when she has acquired the thing she desires. Meaning—I would have married her, Bawn, without love, because they blackened her, the innocent soul, for her mercy to me. But I have learned to love her. She holds my heart against all women. I am not hideous to her."

"And your mother?"

"Is enchanted. We are going to sell Damerstown and live in England. It will give us all a better chance. Good-bye, Miss Bawn, for we shall not meet again."

It made a nine days' wonder when the people heard that Richard Dawson had married Nora Brady; but that was a year later, and Damerstown was shut up and to be let.

Lord and Lady St. Leger still rule at the Abbey, and seem likely to rule for many years, to the joy of their children.

Theobald's wife is keen about her husband's profession, and will not let him leave the army yet, so that we see them only at intervals.

But the old couple are not lonely. My godmother and Uncle Luke have their full measure of happiness. They have, what my dear godmother confessed to me she had not dared to hope for—a child, a boy—brave and beautiful, worthy to succeed his father in time as the Lord St. Leger. There is no bonnier boy in all the countryside except my own, and he is the image of his father, so it is not likely that any child could be just like him. But the young heir fills Aghadoe Abbey with joy and peace. My grandmother told me the other day that the ghosts have not been heard since the child came to banish them.

Katharine Tynan – A Short Biography

Katharine Tynan was born on January 23rd, 1859 into a large family in Clondalkin, County Dublin, Ireland to parents Andrew Cullen Tynan (1829-1905) and Elizabeth O'Reilly (1831- c1869).

The family business was cattle rearing and the farmhouse, set with the mountains for a back drop, was a wonderful world for a young mind to learn and imagine, set out with an orchard at the back, a garden with a sun-dial, a summer-house, a labyrinth of little flower-beds with box borders, a privet hedge, and a great walnut tree.

Initially the young Katharine was slow to learn. She was educated at the Dominican convent school, St Catherine of Sienna, in Drogheda. It appears Katharine had a stubborn streak which inhibited her ability to learn as easily as the school would wish. However she would learn on her own terms and soon began to take her 'forbidden literature', hidden in her clothing, to her loft in a stable hideaway.

Her reading covered everything from Aurora Floyd (her mother failed to approve of this type of book) to "The Mysteries of Paris," by Eugene Sue, some lurid romances of G. W. Reynolds, a set of Maria Edgeworth, "The Poets of the Nation"—eclectic at the very least.

Her father though let her read everything, from "The Wide Wide World" to "Tristram Shandy," from Faber's "Tales of the Angels" to "The Near and the Heavenly Horizons" of Madame de Gasparin. She had books of Longfellow, a Burns of the most complete and unexpurgated, a Milton, a Moore, of course, and the first two volumes of the Corn-hill, where she revelled in Owen Meredith, and "The Great God Pan" of Mrs. Browning.

However until she turned seventeen none of this appeared to point to a literary career. But now that would change and her first verse were written and then printed in a Dublin newspaper.

The good reception to them led to another sonnet being printed in the Spectator. Thereafter the Graphic published several others and even paid a half guinea for the privilege.

By twenty she began to form friendships among those in the Dublin literary circles. The first was Father Russell of The Irish Monthly, the brother of whom was afterwards Lord Russell of Killowen, Lord Chief Justice of England. Through him she made various literary friendships and associations. Lady Russell's sister, Miss Rosa Mulholland, now Lady Gilbert, was an initial object of the young girl's worship.

In 1884 Katharine dispatched herself to London for the first time, and made an abiding friendship when she met Mrs Alice Meynell.

Alice, of course, was an established poet and helped, with her husband Wilfred, to publish many other poets. The following year Wilfred arranged for the publication of her first volume of poems, "Louise de la Vallière" (1885). The book brought her new friends: William Rossetti, Christina Rossetti, Cardinal Newman, and Cardinal Manning.

At about this timer Katharine became a close friend of Gerard Manley Hopkins and also formed a growing attachment to William Butler Yeats (who, it is rumoured, may have proposed marriage and been rejected), and later she became friendly with the correspondent of the Irish Nationalist and excellent poet Francis Ledwidge.

Katharine published a further book of poems "Shamrock" in 1887.

Returning to Ireland, she found herself welcomed into a literary circle, of which W. B. Yeats, "A. E." Russell, and Douglas Hyde were members. They would meet at the houses of Dr. Sigerson, John and Ellen O'Leary (the old Fenian chief and his sister), and Johnson of Ballykilbeg.

In 1889 she was back in London with the Meynells. Katharine remembered an historic evening at Lord Russell's house in Harley Street, when Gladstone, Lord Randolph Churchill and Charles Stewart Parnell, a stalwart in the cry for Irish Home Rule, were met together (Parnell was recovering his career as leader of the Irish Parliamentary Party after a forger Richard Pigott had supplied forgeries to the Times implicating Parnell in murder. Parnell was exonerated and Pigott committed suicide). Mr. Gladstone buried himself in a corner with an elderly lady, an old crony of his, and Lord Randolph disappeared early, and Mr. Parnell turned from the adulation of the crowd to startled surprise at the sight of one young Irishwoman who worshipped him and always would.

As she gathered friends and contacts into her life her literary output began to gather pace. Katharine had begun to write prose for the Speaker and for the Scots and National Observer. The noted writer and poet William Ernest Henley was a great admirer and he praised her work, giving her an inscribed copy of his book The Song of the Sword, inscribed "Katharine Tynan, Sorori in Arte," and others of his books including Hawthorn and Lavender.

In 1892 she married happily to Henry Albert Hinkson, he was almost six years younger, a fellow writer and a barrister. They moved to England, records give their address as 9 Loughfield Road, Ealing, in London, where the marriage produced five children although two were to tragically die in infancy.

In her growing literary efforts she would now usually write under the name Katharine Tynan Hinkson, or a similar variation.

By 1894 her output was prolific and was ranged from poetry to novels to short stories. It would later include a biography and a large amount of editing including the four volume "Cabinet of Irish Literature," a new edition of which she prepared for Blackie's, of Glasgow. She was also a reviewer, and contributed to many magazines.

Katharine's later volumes of verse are those of a natural and spontaneous order characteristic of the Irish muse.

In reviewing "A Cluster of Nuts," (1894) a writer for the Athenæum wrote: "Mrs Hinkson is a lyric poet, and her prose, like her verse, is near to the heart of nature, sweet with the smell of fresh grass and flowering thorn, and warm with a tender sympathy that embraces all things that live and die; but that goes out more fully to trees and fields and summer skies than to men and women." This was doubtless true at the time, and as far as it went, but Mrs. Hinkson has written much since then; her human relationships have increased, and no one can read her child poetry without feeling that her human sympathy is keen, tender, warm, and constant. Many mother-hearts will find expression in "The Meeting," "The Mother," and "The Desire." Devotional feeling makes much of her verse religious in the best sense, and spirituality of thought often imparts the lustre which transfigures.

In 1912 the family returned to Claremorris, County Mayo, when her husband was appointed magistrate there a post he held until his early death in 1919.

She is now also sometimes grouped amongst the War Poets of the First World War. Her experience was not direct but as a Mother with one son serving in France and another in Palestine, the emotions, fears and doubts are expressed in a beautiful heart-felt way.

Involved in the Irish Literary Revival, Tynan expressed concern for feminist causes, the poor, and the effects of World War I in her work. She also meditated on her Catholic faith.

She is said to have written over 100 novels, 12 collections of short stories, plays and many volumes of enduring poetry. Katharine's talents also extended in total to five volumes of autobiography.

Katharine Tynan Hinkson died at age 72 on 2 April 1931 in Kensal Green, London.

Katharine Tynan – A Concise Bibliography

Louise de la Vallière (1885) poems
Shamrocks (1887)
Ballads & Lyrics (1891)
Irish Love-Songs (1892)
A Cluster of Nuts, Being Sketches Among My Own People (1894)
Cuckoo Songs (1894)

Miracle Plays (1895)
The Land of Mist and Mountain (1895)
The Way of a Maid (1895)
Three Fair Maids, or the Burkes of Derrymore (c.1895)
An Isle in the Water (1896)
The Golden Lily (1899)
The Dear Irish Girl (1899)
Oh, What a plague is Love! (1900)
Her Father's Daughter (1900)
Poems (1901)
A Daughter of the Fields (1901)
A King's Woman (1902)
Love of Sisters (1902)
The Great Captain: A Story of the Days of Sir Walter Raleigh (1902)
The Handsome Quaker, and other Stories (1902)
The Adventures of Carlo (1903)
The Luck of the Fairfaxes (1904)
A Daughter of Kings (1905)
Innocencies (1905) poems
For the White Rose (1905)
A Little Book for Mary Gill's Friends (1905)
The Story of Bawn (1906)
The Yellow Domino (1906)
Book of Memory (1906)
Dick Pentreath (1906)
The Cabinet of Irish Literature. (4 volumes) (1906) editor, expansion of work by Charles Read
The Rhymed Life of St Patrick (1907)
Twenty-One poems, selected by W. B. Yeats
A Little Book of XXIV Carols (1907)
Father Mathew (1908) biography of Theobald Mathew
Experiences (1908)
A Union of Hearts (1908)
The House of the Crickets (1908)
Ireland (1909)
A Little Book for John O'Mahony's Friends (1909)
The Book of Flowers (1909) with Frances Maitland
Mary Gray(1909)
A Girl of Galway
The Rich Man
A Red, Red Rose (c.1910)
Heart O' Gold or the Little Princess
The Story of Cecelia (1911)
New Poems (1911)
Princess Katharine (1911)
Twenty-five Years: Reminiscences (1913)
Irish Poems (1913)
The Wild Harp (1913) poetry anthology, editor.
A Mesalliance (1913)
The Daughter of the Manor (1914)
A Shameful Inheritance (1914)
The Flower of Peace (1914) poems

Mary Beaudesert, V. S. (1915)
Flower of Youth (1915) poems
The Curse of Castle Eagle (1915)
The House of the Foxes (1915) novel
Joining the colours (1916)
Lord Edward: A Study in Romance (1916)
The Holy War (Great War Poems) (1916)
The Middle Years (1916)
Margery Dawe (1916)
Late Songs (1917)
Herb O'Grace (1918) (Poems)
The Sad Years (1918) tribute to Dora Sigerson
The Years of the Shadow (1919)
The Honourable Molly (1919)
Denys the Dreamer (1920)
The Handsome Brandons (1921)
Bitha's Wonderful Year (1922)
The Wandering Years (1922)
Evensong (1922)
White Ladies (1922)
A Mad Marriage (1922)
Memories (1924)
Life in the Occupied Area (1925)
The Man from Australia (1925)
The Wild Adventure (1927)
Twilight Songs (1927)
The Face in the Picture (1927)
Haroun of London (1927)
Pat, the Adventurer (1928)
The Respectable Lady (1928)
The River (1929)
Castle Perilous (1929)
The Squire's Sweetheart (1930)
Denise the Daughter (1930)
Collected Poems (1930)
The Admirable Simmons (1930)
The Forbidden Way (1931)
Philippa's Lover (1931)
A Lonely Maid (1931)
The Story of Our Lord (1932)
The Other Man (1932)
An International Marriage (1933)
Londonderry Air (1935)
The Briar Bush Maid
A Little Radiant Girl
A Passionate Pilgrim
Maxims
A Girls Song"

www.ingramcontent.com/pod-product-compliance
Lightning Source LLC
Chambersburg PA
CBHW071715040426
42446CB00011B/2078